GRAPHIC GAMES

GRAPHIC GAMES

FROM PATTERN TO COMPOSITION

VICTOR BAUMGARTNER

PRENTICE-HALL, INC., ENGLEWOOD CLIFFS, NEW JERSEY 07632

Library of Congress Cataloging in Publication Data

BAUMGARTNER, VICTOR.
  Graphic games.

  1. Graphic arts—Technique. 2. Repetitive patterns
(Decorative arts) 3. Symmetry (Art) 4. Composition
(Art) I. Title.
NC1000.B3 1983   745.4   82-16137
ISBN 0-13-363333-0

Editorial/production supervision: Hilda Tauber
Interior and cover design: Suzanne Behnke
Cover illustration by Victor Baumgartner
Manufacturing buyer: Harry P. Baisley

GRAPHIC GAMES: FROM PATTERN TO COMPOSITION
by Victor Baumgartner

Printed in the United States of America

10 9 8 7 6 5 4 3 2 1

Frontispiece: Contemporary Pakistani textile. Appliqué and
embroidery with mirror embelishment.

ISBN 0-13-363333-0

PRENTICE-HALL INTERNATIONAL, INC., *London*
PRENTICE-HALL OF AUSTRALIA PTY. LIMITED, *Sydney*
EDITORA PRENTICE-HALL DO BRASIL, LTDA., *Rio de Janeiro*
PRENTICE-HALL CANADA INC., *Toronto*
PRENTICE-HALL OF INDIA PRIVATE LIMITED, *New Delhi*
PRENTICE-HALL OF JAPAN, INC., *Tokyo*
PRENTICE-HALL OF SOUTHEAST ASIA PTE. LTD., *Singapore*
WHITEHALL BOOKS LIMITED, *Wellington, New Zealand*

THIS BOOK IS FOR CHRIS
AND SHE KNOWS ALL THE REASONS WHY

CONTENTS

PREFACE

GRAPHIC GAMES is an activated text on pattern thinking and the two-dimensional surface. The result of eighteen years of teaching and using the methods described, it was undertaken in response to the urging of my students who wanted a practical and theoretical textbook that would make available continued self-study and provide a forum for the exchange and growth of ideas.

The idea began with my interest in indigenous arts, particularly the designs of the West Coast tribes of the Americas. As a child I used to wander about the old Washington State Historical Museum, enthralled by the collection of Indian artifacts—bowls, ladles, rattles, clothes, baskets, a canoe. At that time of course I had no notions about design organization, and was not aware whether the surfaces were symmetrical or asymmetrical, or how the color was placed and why. Though I did not analyze these objects, I would admire them hour after hour, and frequently I copied parts into my early art productions because I found them attractive.

Later, under the influence of art schools, my pantheon of the gods and goddesses of aesthetics expanded rapidly. I discovered Paul Klee, Henri Matisse, Piero della Francesca, and many others, while my interest in Oriental art continued and my interest in tribal arts increased.

At one point it struck me as odd that I could like so many different art expressions, that I could respond with equal intensity to a finely designed ancient textile or an early Italian fresco, to a Cezanne painting or a classical Japanese house. Eventually I realized that it was not the particulars of style or material handling that were compelling, but the way in which these factors worked internally—how they came together. Indeed their abstract qualities went beyond time and place. With that awareness I could look back at the museum objects of my early experience and see them in an entirely different way.

Meanwhile, my interest in Indian art had extended north to Alaska and south to Peru. Aside from the immediate sensuous attraction many of the things

had for me, I was absorbed in amateur research into their production. I found myself looking in a new way, tracing certain kinds of recurrent visual themes and structures from culture to culture, and finding correspondences in objects from all over the world.

Later, in California, when I came to teach two- and three-dimensional design, forms from other cultures than our own were used not for images and shapes that could be copied, but for the clarity of the structural relations within their design. We also wanted to avoid the rift between fine art and craft—so-called "high" art and "low" art—that interferes with judgment based on direct perception. Through much looking, note taking, thinking, and doing, certain ideas distilled themselves out as central and proved their workability as a common design language in the classroom and in my own work. Using the processes involved, students made design applications ranging from floor tiles to floor plans, from specific designs for commercial manufacture to one-of-a-kind handmade pieces, as well as being stimulated to individual expression in drawing, painting, and collage.

Eventually, as more ideas were tried, revised, or discarded, some shaped themselves into a useful sequence of theoretical problems in surface design. They make up the working sections of this book. The central idea is that pattern is a rational basis for reordering random visual impressions into comprehensible and communicable design structures. In Chapter 1 we lay the foundation of Pattern: equal and contained interactions of shapes. Chapter 2 progresses through the rhythmic emphasis of Distribution of pattern-like elements. In Chapter 3 we expand to the dynamics of Composition. Throughout, repetition is the connection—the theme common to all.

This idea of surface design as systems of pattern relationships is developed through a series of "games" played with simple elements which move from the direct approach of repetition in pattern creation to the inner complexities of composition. Each game is a fundamental step in thinking relationally about the two-dimensional surface, and each is capable of being interpreted and extended in many ways. Each game-name is related to the continuing development in complexity of thinking about the surface as the theme is brought to its logical conclusion in composition.

A basic attitude expressed in the text is that all parts of the field or picture plane are of equal importance in developing visual coherence and subsequent meaning. All elements on the surface are interacting, question and answer, thrust and return; and contextual relations are what give form and plastic validity to the result. Connections—what happens *between* elements—are essential.

The aim here is not a method of producing one, two, or three separate designs for some immediate purpose, but of developing a process of approaching the surface through which design after design results from a working *through* rather than a working *to*. Since the concern is with relationships rather than with isolated entities, and everything shown and discussed at one place belongs to everything else, it is artificial to talk about one thing at a time. But to talk about everything at once would lead to total confusion. This problem has been faced by establishing a sequence going from simple basics to complex results, with a certain amount of textual repetition front to back. Key illustrations are discussed more than once and are presented from different points of view in differing contexts to bring together the thought processes involved.

Since pattern structure is used as the basis of the design process, traditional frames of reference used when discussing surface dynamics are minimized. Figure-field, center-of-interest, harmony, balance, and so on, usually gone into in other books, are mentioned here after the fact or to stress a point. They are fundamental qualities, certainly, but not fundamentally operative qualities. They seem more the result of action rather than an action.

Nor are techniques central to the content of this book. A brief description of the method used accompanies an illustration when it is needed to clarify the design of whatever is shown. The games may be played with the simplest materials, and require only a modicum of technical skill in order to understand the design ideas in them. My emphasis, always, is on the idea that may necessitate a given technique rather than the technique itself.

In this book, furthermore, I have strived to avoid qualitative evaluations, for art criticism belongs to another area of appreciation with its own methods and procedures.

I am grateful to the students who have given me permission to include as examples their solutions to various surface design problems. I also wish to thank the individuals and institutions that have taken the time to answer my questions and have graciously allowed me to reproduce materials in their collections. They include The American Museum of Natural History, New York City; The Buffalo Museum of Science, Buffalo, New York; The Cooper-Hewitt Museum, New York City; The Denver Art Museum, Denver, Colorado; The Field Museum of Natural History, Chicago, Illinois; The National Gallery of Art, Washington, D.C.; The Seattle Art Museum, Seattle, Washington; and The University of British Columbia Museum of Anthropology, Vancouver, B.C., Canada. I am also grateful to Dover Publications, Inc., New York, for their kind permission to use several illustrations from their book *African Designs from Traditional Sources* by Geoffrey Williams. If no source is mentioned, the material is from my personal collection.

GRAPHIC GAMES

INTRODUCTION

HOW TO USE
THE BOOK

FIGURE 1
Games with pattern tiles and tools.

The two-dimensional surface is the playing field for the games in this book. On this field design elements are moved around—*manipulated*—from position to position to learn about pattern and composition structures and how their visual effects can be controlled. The *how* and *why* of all moves is illustrated by diagrams and by examples of many different finished designs.

Chapters 1, 2, and 3 should be taken up in their order of presentation. Chapter 1 (Pattern) states the major themes and introduces the idea of a strong symmetrical surface organization. Chapter 2 (Distribution) produces surfaces that are more intricate in their asymmetrical rhythms. The working structures of both are synthesized in Chapter 3 (Composition). The three chapters should be read and used in this sequence because all the work is based on the premises introduced in the simple games of Pattern. They are the foundation for developing ideas in Distribution and Composition, and very little of the content of those parts can be understood if the Pattern games are not played first.

MATERIALS

All the games can be played using simple materials. Use any means available to draw a grid with a fine but legible line on smooth finish white paper or board. Ruler and pencil, carefully used, work well; a T-square and triangle work better. They give greater accuracy and control, which are important in maintaining equal increments and areas, for grids must be precisely drawn. Graph paper is useful for sketches but not necessary for full-scale or finished work.

Black felt-tipped pens are a versatile and easy drawing tool available in a variety of nib widths good for sketching and fine line work. They have the advantage of being clean and convenient and are recommended for those who have little experience with drawing ink, gouache, or other wet media.

The following is a generous list of the supplies you will need. Items may be added, subtracted, or substituted for with comparable materials. It is always economically wise to buy the best quality items affordable since they function better and last longer. What works and is comfortable to use is the best criterion for choice.

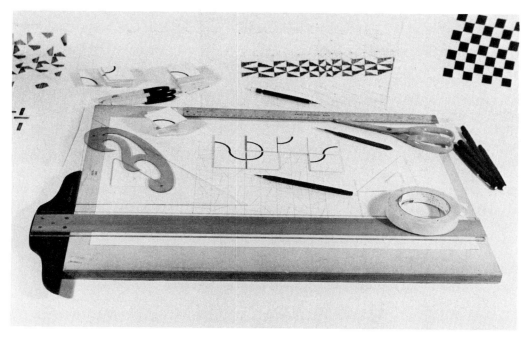

FIGURE 2
Tools for work set-up.

1

A good size drawing board; light weight hollow-core is best

Heavy weight white paper with a smooth, not glossy, finish

A roll of tracing paper of medium weight

Graph paper; five squares to the lineal inch is a good size

Black and middle value gray construction paper

A flexible steel, cork backed, 18-inch ruler

Clear plastic 30°-60° triangle

Clear plastic 45° triangle

A T-square to fit the drawing board size

Drafting tape

Transparent tape

Push pins

Drawing pencils, including 4H, 2H, H or F, HB, and 2B

A pencil sharpener

Felt-tipped pens, black, with various nib widths from fine to broad

Rubber cement

White glue

Matt knife

Paper shears

A set of mechanical drawing drafting tools, if possible

WORKING METHODS

Keep all working methods as simple as possible and concentrate on understanding and developing the design ideas in the games. Working techniques have a happy way of suggesting themselves, and the best manner of getting the ideas down on the page will evolve with the ideas. Arrange to have a work space with good light that can be left set up, so you can avoid the annoying interference of continually setting up and taking down.

Play all the games in black and white, or in black, white, and gray. Color should not be used, particularly in beginning exercises, since it introduces complexities that while certainly interesting, may prove beyond control before the basic structures in dark-light are understood. Once the sequence of games has been worked through in value only, the enrichment of color may be attempted.

Since so much of the work is based upon repetition of a single design unit, it is advisable to cut multiples of that unit out of black paper and position them on the grid lines drawn on white paper. Outlin-

FIGURE 3
Stencil

ing each unit and filling it in for preparatory work, or to get an idea of what the area will look like as a whole, is very time consuming and really not worth the effort involved. By using shapes cut from paper, results can be achieved quickly and can be changed at once if they are unsatisfactory. When the overall design is established in its final arrangement, individual shapes can be permanently positioned on the grid with rubber cement or white glue, or—and a better method—transferred to another grid by drawing and filling in with a felt marker for a finished piece.

Another useful and time-saving device is a stencil (Figure 3). Cut the outline of the carefully drawn shape out of heavy paper with a sharp cutting tool (shears will not work here). Carefully key it to the exact measure of a single grid unit so it can be used accurately over the surface, and draw the outline of the shape in each grid unit. Later the shapes can be filled in with felt pen, gouache, or ink. A stencil is a necessity when doing gradations of value in smudged graphite.

USING A GRID

A grid is by no means a new invention and its use in this text is not unique. Squaring off an area is an ancient device for organization. It was used by early Polynesian navigators and is still used by archaeologists, architects, cartographers, typographers, artists,

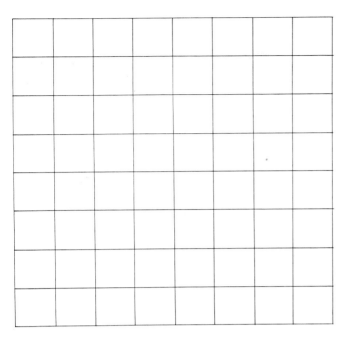

FIGURE 4
The grid.

tinuous static units but create more than one shape on the page when aligned. The square never moves, and when aligned becomes the definition of each succeeding square. These qualities—static form, mutually defining edges, and right angles—create the fundamental framework necessary for playing the games.

A checkerboard is not a grid and should not be treated as one. It is a basic pattern structure based upon the grid with one dark square alternating with one light square. The difference between the linear framework of the grid and the dark-light development of the checkerboard pattern should be clearly understood. The grid is the linear support; the checkerboard is the dark-light pattern based upon it. It takes one dark and one light square to make a repeat. This combination, when alternated in succeeding rows, whether vertical or horizontal, makes the checkerboard. The simplest pattern is made from the same unit repeated in each grid square, but a single grid unit is not always an entire repeat; often many units must be combined into larger units depending upon the variations in positions of shapes within the units. A *repeat* is always referred to as *that area that joins and contains exactly the same material as the areas next to it on all sides.* Like a checkerboard, a repeat should not be confused with the grid or one of its individual units, and the manner in which they function together when plotting the layout of a surface.

and designers. Frequently it is used as a design device or an image in itself. The grid is an obvious structural diagram: equidistant parallel lines set against each other, intersecting at 90° angles, making a web. Each unit of the web contains some visual activity related to adjoining units, the sum making up a completely defined surface. Its most obvious statement is in pattern where the insistence on the rhythm of repetition is dominant. As the work becomes more complex in composition the visual influence of the grid lessens until it is absorbed into the design. Its appearance, or use, is nearly subliminal in some of the illustrations in the latter part of the book.

The squared grid, in which each of the four sides of the unit is equal in measure to the others, is not the only linear grid but it is the simplest. Nearly all pattern applications throughout the world are developed on it, or their structures can be interpreted through it. This book employs the squared grid as the neutral playing field for all the games because it establishes a common frame of reference and is the means through which they become interchangeable. A grid composed of rectangles, triangles, or hexagons has already established an active pattern response. The static square, with its four equal sides and four right angles, allows a unit to be manipulated in many ways because it has edge relationships and it stays put.

Circles cannot be used. They center, have no edge or angle relationships, and do not repeat as con-

FIGURE 5
The checkerboard.

How many units to use and how large they should be depends upon the character of the pattern and the repeat area necessary to realize it. Patterns should have at least three full repeats across and three down. This is considered a minimum when making the relationship between them clear since the surface activity is distributed through a series of connections rather than a single join. For the games, a convenient beginning size would be a grid composed of $1\frac{1}{2} \times 1\frac{1}{2}$ inch units, eight across and eight down, for a total of sixty-four squares. A larger number of units can be used if desired, or their size may be increased or decreased, but a unit that is less than 1×1 inch makes an uncomfortably tight area and is difficult to work with. A square format is most effective; it concentrates attention within the field and avoids the problem of a dynamic horizontal or vertical movement in the field itself, which is preferable for beginning games.

DESIGNING SHAPES

If the grid is the architectural framework, certainly shapes are the bricks and mortar of the design building, and the interrelations between the two establish the basic construction of pattern and composition. The idea of shape interaction is central in design thinking because it is never the single shape that has to be considered but shapes in combination. Shapes and the manner in which they are manipulated over the foundation of the grid establish the primary relationships of the design and give a distinct character to the surface—whether it bristles with sharp angles or undulates with curves. A shape in isolation may have as many meanings and associations as a single word, a single color, or one note played on a piano. It does not have a specific definition until it is arranged with other shapes and is seen in the relationships of dark-light and proximity. All beginning work in Pattern is concerned with this problem in surface design.

There is an entire vocabulary describing the associations attached to shapes and their interpretation: "anthropomorphic," "zoomorphic," "natural" or "abstract" shapes, and so on. Many terms are elusive and cannot be specifically defined, but most fit into the two large inclusive divisions "organic" and "geometric," and these are the categories that will be used here. *Organic* refers to models found in nature, or those shapes that have a strong reference to plants and animals or patterns of growth. *Geometric* refers to the standard planar figures: square, triangle, hexagon, prism, and so forth, or shape variations based on them or on combinations of them. The two categories are not mutually exclusive, and the risk of confusion when they overlap is well worth it for the richness of shape variety that can be produced. Organic or geometric shapes may be either symmetric or asymmetric in design. Symmetry or the lack of it is not their basic characteristic, which is the feeling generated by the shape's relation to its source or original model.

To become aware of shapes and build a visual vocabulary of them, it is absolutely necessary to draw

FIGURE 6
Mbala discharge-printed cloth pattern, Congo-Kinshana.

FIGURE 7
Bushongo embroidered cloth pattern, Congo-Kinshana.

FIGURE 8
Bushman rock painting from the Tsibab
ravine, South-West Africa.

FIGURE 9
Woven mat bird design
from the lower Congo area.

FIGURE 10
Beaten pattern on brass sculpture, Dahomey.
From *African Designs from Traditional Sources* by Geoffrey
Williams. © 1971 Dover Publications, Inc., New York.

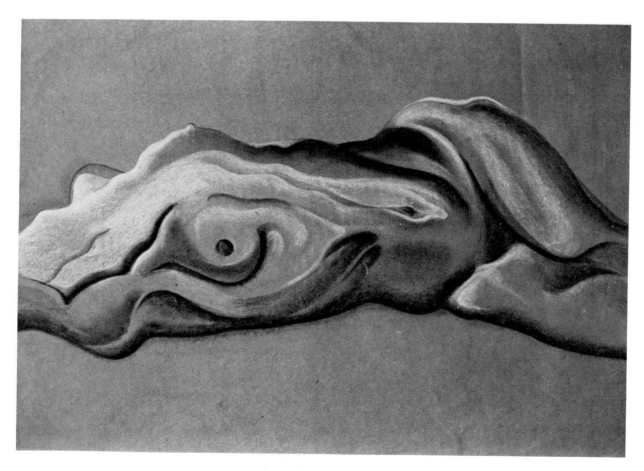

FIGURE 11
Figure drawing.

6

INTRODUCTION

extensively from models such as bones, shells, the human figure, leaves and other natural objects, from geometric forms, and from the imagination. Identifying the parts that compose the whole, and the connections between them in the model, is required groundwork for creating shapes. Pencil, pen, and paper are the only working tools needed to make analytic sketches—neither fancy nor finished drawings—but simplifications and abstractions of shapes revealed by careful looking. The photograph of an animal skull shown in Figure 12 is full of complexities and might seem the wrong thing to choose as a model for the source of a few simple shapes. However, it is not necessary to use everything seen—all the shape information the skull contains—at once. Related parts may be isolated and used effectively. For example, the area around the eye socket, shown enlarged in Figure 13, may be further simplified to a few shapes, some regular and some eccentric in outline. When this drawing process is carried out with many different models literally hundreds of different shapes are the result. A designer must keep eye and mind in constant response to the visual materials, not thinking about methods of producing a pretty drawing, not engaging in a determined search for usable shapes to apply to this or that pattern, but concentrating on the idea of analyzing the salient characteristics of the model and the manner in which they fit together.

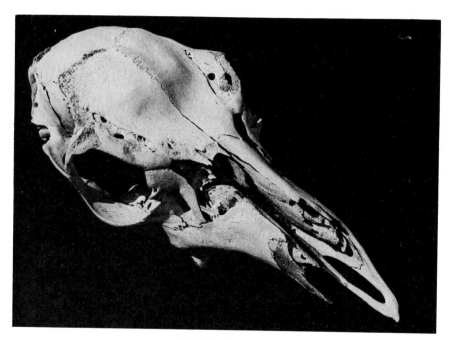

FIGURE 12
Animal skull, photograph.

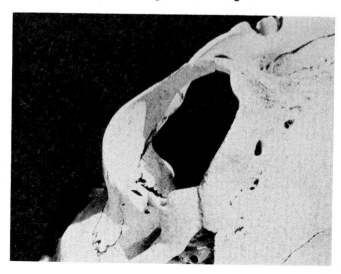

FIGURE 13
Detail of Figure 12, enlarged.

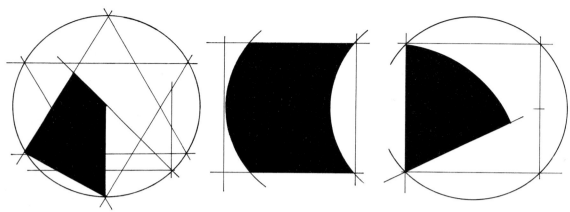

FIGURE 14
Geometric shape variations.

The same open method should be used when handling geometric shapes. Considerable experimentation with compass, protractor, ruler, and pencil will yield a variety of shapes based on circles, squares, triangles, and other geometric planes. By dividing planes, using portions of them, cutting into them, and so on, we can produce many configurations derived from the original models.

Fantasy drawings, notations of images that occur freely in the mind's eye, are another valuable source of shape ideas. This is random drawing with no particular point in mind, and is free of any restriction to make a drawing that resembles any model other than itself. In fantasy drawing we are graphically describing a state of mind rather than an object. Fantasy drawing, such as that shown in Figure 15, could be called creative doodling with the hand and mind simultaneously wandering across the page, letting whatever may occur do so. This method and the method of analytical drawing from models balance and reinforce each another.

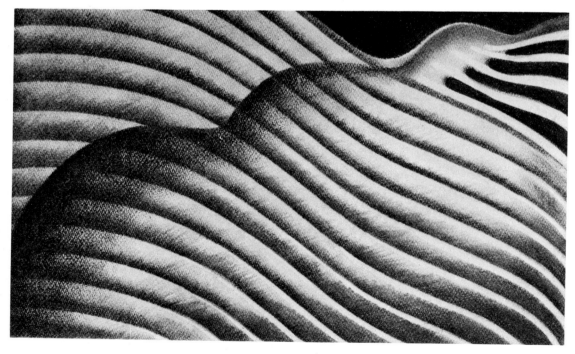

FIGURE 15
Fantasy drawing.

After a session of making drawings, set them aside for a day or two. Later they can be seen from a fresh viewpoint and, by comparing various kinds of drawings, used as a source for further shape invention.

Often design students complain that they do not know what they are looking *for* in such comparative searching, and they object when told that there is nothing predetermined to be found in it, but that it is a process of uncovering linkages and finding relationships in the accumulation of drawn images. However, this method of learning by search, with its occasional frustrations, gives one necessary experience in direct work with visual material and analysis. The benefits of such experimentation are an immediate increase in awareness of shapes, a gain in understanding how to create and control them, and a spontaneously produced inventory of many shapes that can be used in pattern and composition structures.

A foundation of personal visual experiences, continually being enlarged with more work, is laid down in drawing-analysis exercises upon which one builds confidence and selectivity in seeing and interpreting. The relationship between things seen and drawn becomes more refined; looking becomes seeing. All sources of design idea stimulation become areas of intelligent study rather than models for mindless copying. Geometric shapes can be appreciated for their directness and clarity, organic shapes for their connotation and associations. Either organic or geometric shapes may be used in any of the games, but carefully planned geometric shapes are often more successful and should be used for beginning exercises in Pattern, Distribution, and Composition, where the emphasis is put upon understanding the surface as a whole and the relationships that make it so. All shapes should be easily comprehensible, of the utmost simplicity, and have greater interest in their possibilities of combination rather than in themselves. First design attempts invariably produce shapes that are complicated or fussy, and extensive trial and error has to be experienced before simple workable shapes are evolved. It is difficult to simplify and give up an attractive effect in an individual shape that will not work in combination, but it must be done. Any shape so handsome that it seems complete and satisfying in itself has to be looked upon with suspicion—chances are that it will be too complicated to combine well.

Three examples are shown in Figure 17. The first is a simple shape because it cannot be broken into its component parts. It is contained. The second and third are compound shapes that can be separated into simple shapes; they are made up of more than one part. Avoid compound shapes until enough work has been done with simple shapes to see how quickly the

FIGURE 16
Appliqued costume. Ibo, Nigeria.
Courtesy, Field Museum of Natural History, Chicago.

surface complicates itself when shapes are put into combination. Whenever a shape appears too complex to use test it by cutting it out of black paper in multiples and moving them around on the grid. Their grid relationship, potential combinations, readability, dark-light interchange, becomes clear immediately, and the design of the shape can be readily altered, if necessary, by some judicious snipping with a pair of shears. Pencil sketches are rarely useful at this stage; they are too slow and do not show enough.

FIGURE 17
Simple and compound shapes.

Simplicity is stressed because shapes cannot be used by themselves. They are cut to fit a grid unit and when placed in it a balancing shape is automatically created. This dark-light exchange of shapes is called the *design unit,* and combinations of the design unit become the *repeat*. Design units merge at the common edge defined by the grid and still more shapes appear in the repeat. Complexities develop immediately in the process of combining and are much easier to control if the initial moves are simple.

A pattern based on a symmetrical shape resembling an ax-head is found, with many variations, on ancient pots and textiles throughout the world—the Orient, the Americas, and Africa. It can be used as a good example of the bonding of grid and shape to show how the grid becomes absorbed into the completed surface as a passive support. The ax-head is

pleasing in its simplicity and balance. Designed to interlock with itself at a 90° angle, or half-turn, the conjoined shapes are mutually defining at their common edges. The large size of the shape and its interlocking design, in this configuration, limit the possibilities of many varied positions, but its relation to the grid is worth examination.

The pattern could be diagrammed as a series of overlapping circles, as shown in Figure 20. To arrive at the same pattern as that shown in Figure 20, pairs of lines are subtracted from alternating circles which relate to an underlying grid formed at the points where the four circles meet. Rather than starting in this roundabout manner, with its limitations, a simpler and more versatile method is shown in the following diagrams where elements are first simplified and then amplified by the interaction of grid support and shape movement.

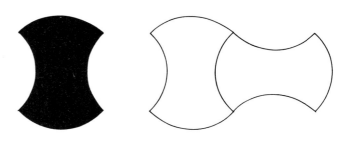

FIGURE 19
Ax-head shape and ax-head interlock.

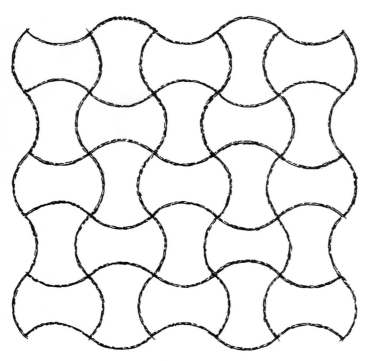

FIGURE 18
All-over linear ax-head pattern.

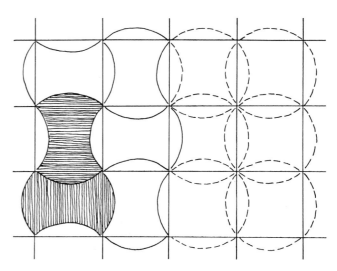

FIGURE 20
Ax-head circle to grid conversion.

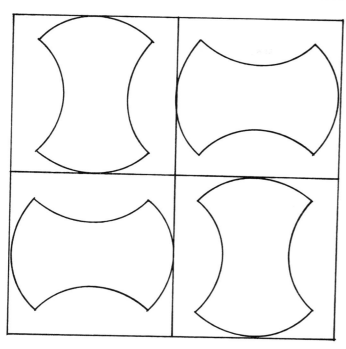

FIGURE 21
Ax-head, contained in grid.

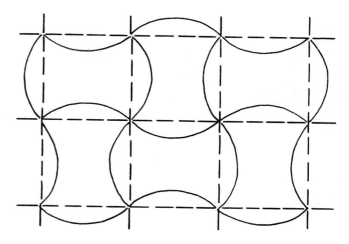

FIGURE 23
Ax-head, shape to fit grid.

If each shape is contained completely within the grid unit, the effect of the complete surface is quite different from how it appears when the shape is seen as part of a joining series—not complete in itself, but dependent upon adjacent units to complete it. Aligning the grid units, turning each one 90 degrees, completes the surface, and the pattern result can be understood as a series of turns or rotations of the shape on the grid. Thus, the actual shape used is that shown on the right in Figure 22, which when turned in alternating grid units produces the familiar ax-head pattern shown in Figure 23.

To carry the idea of simplification of the pattern elements still further, the ax-head is reduced to a primary part—a quarter circle—shown in Figure 24. Reversing the dark-light placement creates two complementary aspects of the same shape. Rotating the shape within the grid unit produces the diagram shown on the left in Figure 25; utilizing a value reversal, the ax-head pattern appears, now with strong cross-diagonal movements, as shown on the right in the figure. This analysis takes the shape down to its simplest component and fully involves the grid to produce a pattern through dark-light shape manipulation. The first analysis produces the limited result of a variation of the grid structure. The possibilities of combination increase as the shape is simplified; they are no longer restricted to making an ax-head figure, but many others as well. The ax-head becomes a part in a series of combinations, some of which are shown in Figure 26.

Shape and grid are interdependent. Whether the relationship between them is in a symmetrical or asymmetrical balance, shapes moving against each other over the fixed grid create the surface in either Pattern, Distribution, or Composition. This contained movement—contained by the control of the grid—establishes the balance of tensions between the active movement of shapes and the static support of the grid.

A shape has to be designed to fit and unite with the grid unit; shapes that do not make edge contact will "float" on the ground, and are sometimes used just for that purpose. However, a floating shape that occupies less than 25 percent of the ground area will not give a convincing dark-light exchange, and the surface will tend to spot out and not adapt to pattern manipulations. Conversely, a shape that occupies

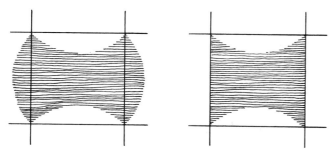

FIGURE 22
Ax-head, shape on grid.

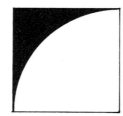

FIGURE 24
Ax-head, quarter-circle reduction.

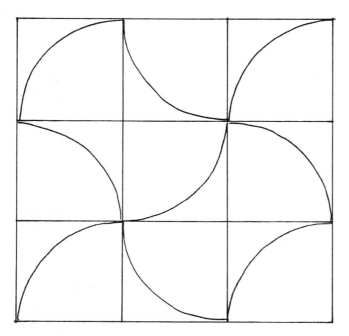

FIGURE 25
Ax-head, all-over web.

that the content of the design is realized in the relationship of its composing elements and that content is inseparable from the method of its realization, that is, the pattern system that is established and expressed relationally.

A right-angle triangle has been used to illustrate basic moves in most of the games because it is a simple shape without the associations and reactions of liking or not liking abstracted birds or conventionalized butterflies or whatnot, and stress can be put on the formal organizations involved. It is a symmetrical shape, although in some combinations it gives the appearance of asymmetry. It occupies 50 percent of the grid unit area, and in combination with the ground forms a complete design unit in equally balanced dark-light. It contacts the grid on two sides and involves it by cutting it diagonally in two across the center. The possibilities of manipulating this design unit are fully examined and shown in Chapter 1.

Designing a shape that is adaptable to many varying positions is not a matter of placing one thing on a field, but is concerned with the integration of figure-field to create a single impression carved from dark-light interaction. Therefore, the proportionate amounts

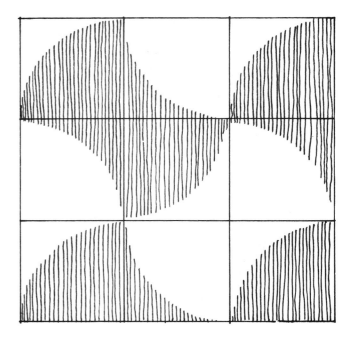

more than 75 percent of the ground will produce reverse spotting when put into combination. Surface equilibrium is achieved by carefully balancing the proportionate interplay of dark and light elements. Shapes that are as contained or complete as the ax-head limit the number of combinations possible. The search is always for the simplest component which, when combined, yields the desired shape and others as well.

In all the games, emphasis is on the how and why of developing a complete surface. For that reason the shapes used in basic examples are kept minimal to avoid the confusion of association or allusion that would detract from the means and methods of basic organizational moves. It is stated over and over again

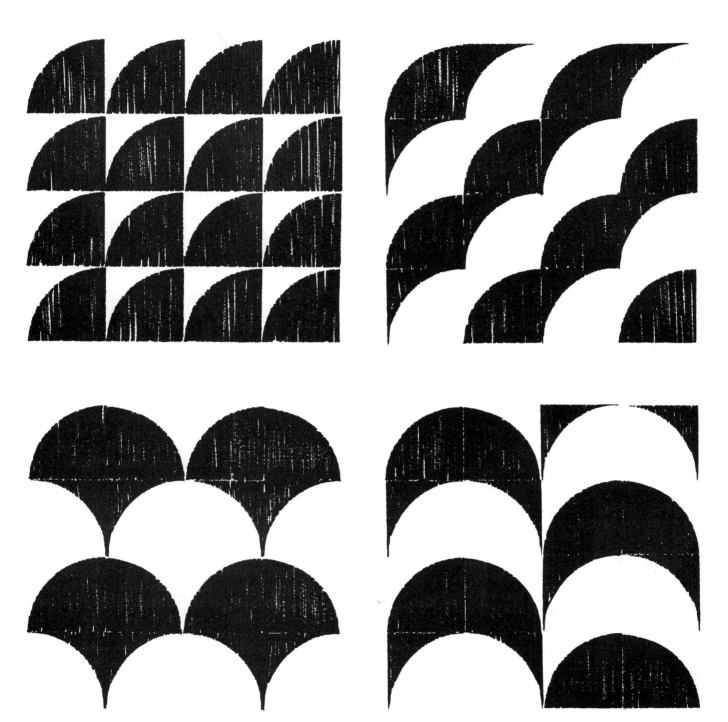

FIGURE 26
Ax-head, variations in shape placement.

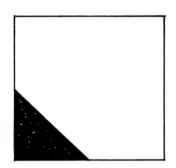

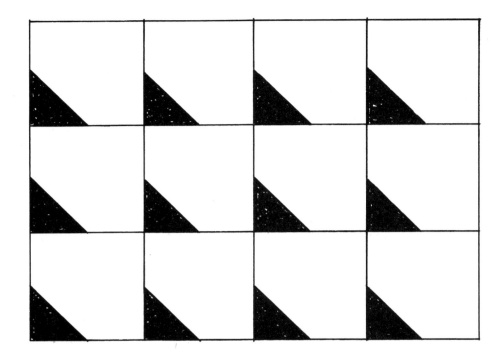

FIGURE 27
Percentage: 25 percent, 75 percent.

of dark-light, their relative percentages, and contact with the edge of the grid unit—and simplicity—are all critical considerations. The matter of shape design and choice for use is important enough to be discussed in each chapter for its particular adaptations and uses there.

Design units in combination create a pattern context which must be kept consistent with itself or no cohesive visual image will be created. It is to this point of cohesiveness that design principles are directed—rhythm, dominance, and so on. At the beginning of a design problem one is always in the limbo of an unrealized idea and cannot start by making an attempt at unity, dominance, tension, or beauty. A visual sensation has to be put down, reacted to, and worked with. Rather than working to a preconceived idea of design, work to the design.

FIGURE 28
Right-angle triangle, right-angle triangle combined, linear.

FIGURE 29
Series of shapes.

PATTERN

EQUAL MOVEMENT OF EQUAL ELEMENTS OVER THE SURFACE

FIGURE 1–1
Carved relief on a Bushongo
wooden drinking vessel, Congo-Kinshana.
From *African Designs from Traditional Sources* by Geoffrey Williams.
© Dover Publications, Inc., New York.

Pattern is the foundation for all of the work in this book. From the obvious repetition of the classic form of the checkerboard, where elements are reduced to a minimum, to the complexities of composition, in which repetition is visually "felt" and less obviously stated, pattern establishes the fundamental rhythm for organizing a surface. It provides an understandable common denominator which can make otherwise seemingly unequal or opposing material comprehensible in its method of relational development.

Pattern in its initial form is simple and static: the surface is grasped as continuous uniform beats without break or variation in its sequence of movement. It is analogous to time being defined in increments of seconds or minutes, or measured in hours, or to the use of meter and rhyme in verse. Pattern establishes a visual rhythm of repetition that is as basic a support to ordered seeing as rhythm and beat are in producing musical phrases. One may say a "minute-and-a-half" or "an hour-and-a-half" or make whatever groupings of time units of seconds, minutes, or hours that is clear and necessary, yet the basic unit of measure remains constant throughout the variations.

Identification of a single visual element that organizes because it repeats can produce a coherency in what would otherwise seem to be only confusion. In the same sense, what one extrapolates and correlates from random visual materials as salient, as essential, is an activity of pattern making. Identification of the rhythmic relationships—relationships in time, sequence, sameness—is the necessary intellectual effort that must be made in the perceptual process. It provides the thematic basis for interpretation that has at its center the idea that connection, the relationship between the parts, is the basis of making systems of communicable order.

Thought of as a method of re-ordering random visual impressions into sensible order, pattern becomes an expressive form rather than being limited to the traditional definition of a type of decoration or ornament which must be applied to pre-existing forms to complete itself. Although pattern is used in many ornamental ways, that usage is more a by-product of the pleasant effect of patterned surfaces, rather than the cause of pattern. Certainly, the aspect of spontaneous adornment, or simple sensuous visual pleasure in pattern exists. Art expressions from many cultures—Eastern and Western—offer hundreds of delightful examples that can be thought of as pure bouyancy of human spirit and the innate will to embellish. Visually the world would be a very stuffy place without them. However, emphasis here is not on the history of decorative design, but on certain formal qualities and elements relating to pattern structures and the surface. Pattern is the basis, and it is defined in the strict sense of producing an articulated surface of similar elements evenly repeated, as well as in the broad sense of visually comprehending a whole because of the clarity of relations between its parts.

GAME A
PERCENTAGES

A percentage is a portion of a whole, or a matter of proportion, which is the size relation of the parts of a whole. *Percentages* is a game played to explore the importance of shape and size relationships and the dark-light interchange between them, factors that must be considered when making a design unit. The structural idea of Percentages is that of the simultaneous exchange of dark and light in the shape configuration within the design unit. The effect of this exchange on the entire surface can be studied by repeating the unit in an even rhythm without variation—a uniform beat over the surface—to make a pattern.

The dark-light relation is the working material of the pattern, for it is not dark nor light alone that makes the surface, but the joining of their contrasts that becomes an experience of visual union. This dark-light interdependence has often been described as that of a "positive-negative" balance, but since it is impossible to read dark without light and vice-versa, that term seems somewhat flimsy. Shapes are mutually defining and read as a single unit whether the dark or the light occupies a greater percentage of the area within the grid unit. The visual reading is in the single contrast of the two parts; the hyphenated term "dark-light" seems clearly descriptive and will be used rather than "positive-negative." For the purposes of the game it doesn't matter whether the light areas are placed on a dark ground or the other way around, although the convenience of conventional usage usually has dark marks being made on a light surface.

The result of playing Percentages will be a series of simple patterns, all realized on the same size format, but each using a different shape. When the series is complete the patterns can be compared to one another to discover what kinds of shapes and amounts produce what kinds of surfaces. Comparison clearly demonstrates the significant contrasts created when using shapes that have a 50–50 percent balance in dark-light, and when using shapes in a 25–75 percentage balance. The first is an equally distributed alternation of dark-light over the surface while the second emphasizes either dominant dark or light areas and results in an entirely different proportionate reading. To make comparisons is to make necessary design connections and is the reason for always working in a series of designs rather than doing a single piece at a time. Proportionately integrated surfaces are grasped as complete; all the composing elements appear to belong together with no irrelevant visual interferences. Weaker surfaces have composing elements that call attention to themselves and disrupt the organization, slowing the visual search for the whole or fragmenting the impression. A basic question asked when developing a patterned surface is: Do the elements join together and appear as complete and balanced, or do they tend to separate, one visually floating on the surface of the other? The answer is found by making comparisons in a connected sequence of pattern statements.

FIRST MOVES: GRID AND SHAPE RELATIONSHIP

Once you have made some shapes according to the methods discussed in the Introduction, begin to experiment with them. Draw a grid of 1½ or 2 inch units in 2H or 4H pencil on white paper using a T-square and a triangle or other drawing tools. Trial areas can be done on a three by three unit repeat, then expanded to a six by six, or eight by eight size for a better reading.

Transfer the shape, measured to fit the size of the grid unit, to black paper, and by putting several sheets together, cut out multiples of the shape. Align them on the grid, and stand back and look at them. A handy device is to use a thick backing board made of material that can be pinned into; the grid and the shapes can be fastened to it with straight pins and the whole apparatus propped up and viewed from a distance. If space is very limited a reducing glass should be used. Whatever the method, it is important that the work be studied from close and far to make accurate visual judgments. It is likely that changes will have to be made in the shape, and that can be done by cutting directly into it without preliminary drawing.

VARYING SHAPE SIZE AND POSITION

The following illustrations show some methods of experimenting with relative percentages of dark-light shape interaction within the grid unit. Certain of them have been selected and used as all-over patterns to illustrate the idea of comparative criticism. The examples are planned and shown in sequence, which is meant to serve as a model of procedure for all the Pattern games.

Figure 1-2 illustrates a series of four percentage variations on a basic shape. Whether or not the shapes are inherently interesting is not the point, which is that they may become so when combined. The shape second from the left shows an equal balance of exchange of dark-light within the grid unit, which in this case composes the complete design unit. It is 50 percent dark and 50 percent light. The design unit on the left is dominantly light, while that on the right is dominantly dark.

Four closely related patterns are produced with a simple alignment of the design units on the grid—in a one-to-one repetition—and compared for their dark-light exchange in Figure 1-3. The first, in the upper left, is a vertical saw-tooth dark stripe on a light

FIGURE 1–2
Percentage shape sequence.

GAME A: PERCENTAGES

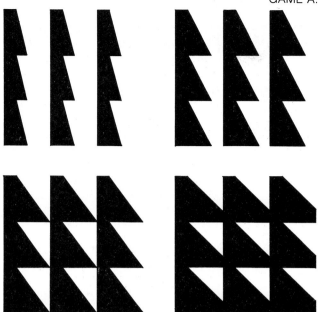

FIGURE 1–3
Percentage pattern sequence.

interact with one another. For example, the pattern shown in the upper right of Figure 1-3 shows an equal amount distribution of dark and light shapes. The observer can at will call up the light areas as dominant, or the dark areas as dominant. After prolonged viewing the dark-light exchange appears to fluctuate—their balance is equal. Certainly there is nothing wrong with less dark and more light in a pattern, or vice-versa, but control of proportion comes through the recognition of the idea that both dark and light must be treated as equally important when constructing a surface. Equal balance is not the ony method of achieving dark-light interaction. The pattern in the lower left of the illustration shows a lesser proportion of light to dark than that shown in the upper right, but it is still possible to visually exchange the dark and light planes more easily than those shown in the saw-tooth stripe.

This discussion of grid alignments, shape control, repetition and what to do and what not to do and look for on the surface can sound very restrictive, if not downright oppressive. Not so, however, when it is actually being done and the relationships come up from the page with an immediate visual impact. Then the possibilities begin to suggest themselves, not only in shape development—and never let a good shape idea pass without making a note of it—but in placement and combinations, and the game becomes exciting and interesting to play.

Continuing the sequence of shape development by giving the shape seen second from the right in Figure 1-2 a quarter-turn counterclockwise and removing a part of it, produces the shape shown at the upper left in Figure 1-4. By lessening the amount of

ground. Usually, the greater the amount of relative light to relative dark, the greater the emphasis will be on the smaller amount, which is true here. The saw-tooth line reads as belonging to dark, not to both dark and light, and tends to minimize the activity of the light area causing it to recede to the position of a supporting field. Whether from the long established habit of reading black letters on a white page, or from drawing with dark marks on a light page, there appears to be an assumption in most viewers that light functions as a support, or a passive receiver for dark; the viewer's attention is drawn to the darks and the surface is read as dark on light. In a specific instance, such as the pattern being discussed, this observation is true; however, in pattern work in general it cannot be substantiated. The pattern shown in the lower right reverses the importance of the dark-light relationship: here triangles of white appear as regularly positioned on a dark field. Although reversed, light on dark, rather than dark on light, the thinking remains the same: that one or the other of the dark-light areas is acting as a passive support to an active figure through which the pattern configuration is recognized. In certain situations this attitude of surface will work, but it does not deal with the central issue of dark-light interchange, or the idea that there is a continuous figure-field fluctuation in which the dark figure becomes the field of a light figure, which in turn exchanges with an adjoining dark. In fact, the figure-field relationship ceases to be as such, and all shapes

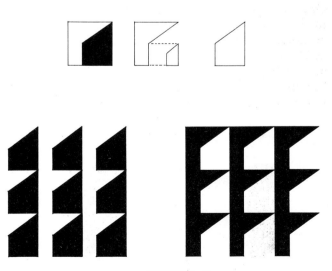

FIGURE 1–4
Percentage shape and pattern sequence with reversal.

dark area the balance of relative percents of dark-light is nearly equalized, and again the shapes begin to merge in a reciprocal exchange between figure and field. An important factor that increases the tension, and therefore the visual exchange between the shapes composing the single design unit, is that by removing part of the dark the increased light area becomes a compound shape made up of the parts shown in the upper right of the illustration. The distinct difference in dark and light configuration that make the one shape creates a contrast and ambiguity of visual importance between the two that is effective in maintaining an integrated dark-light exchange within the design unit. It is based on the same observations made about the continuity of areas that successively define one another rather than the idea of an emphatic reading of a clearly defined and isolated shape on a supporting ground. The pattern made from the new shape is shown at the lower left in the illustration, opposed to another version on the right in which the dark-light is reversed for a complete study comparison.

The dark area is reduced further in Figure 1-5, and taken down to a minimal amount in the design unit shown in the upper right which is also shown organized as a pattern. This figure should be compared to the saw-tooth stripe at the beginning of this sequence since it completes this series of examinations of a basic shape by returning to a pattern in which the dark is stressed in importance by its contrast in proportion to light.

Comparing the figures in the sequence should clarify the point of Percentages since, finally, it must be a visual rather than a verbal definition. Adjusting relative amounts of dark and light in design units based on a common shape, without deviating from a standard method of placement of the completed design unit on the grid structure, gives many different char-

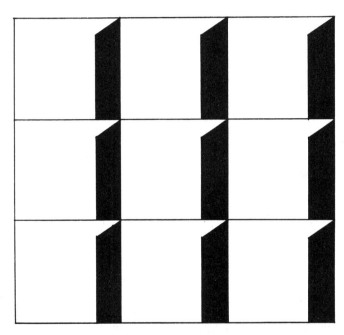

FIGURE 1–5
Percentage shape and pattern sequence, minimal amounts.

FIGURE 1–6
Percentage shape diagram.

acteristics to the final patterned surface: shapes on a supporting field, stripes, all-over pattern, strong directional movement, or contained pattern activity. In all of them the final effect is created by the relative amounts of dark and light. Patterned surfaces may fail for a variety of reasons, but one of the most common is because this primary idea of dark-light interdependence is not carefully considered and concientiously controlled. When the dark shape, for example, is looked upon as independent rather than part of the dark-light combination that makes the design unit, light areas will not receive equal attention and problems are bound to occur when constructing the surface. It is relative amounts of dark and light in combination that create the whole impression.

DEVELOPING DARK-LIGHT INTERCHANGE

A simple demonstration of this interchange and what it can do is the subject of the following set of illustrations (Figures 1-7 to 1-10). To isolate and underscore the point of dark-light interchange, the design material has been taken out of the frame of reference of the right-angled grid for the moment and put into a slightly different context.

FIGURE 1–7
Ashanti "Adinkira" printing stamp pattern, Ghana.
From *African Designs from Traditional Sources* by Geoffrey Williams. © 1971 Dover Publications, Inc., New York.

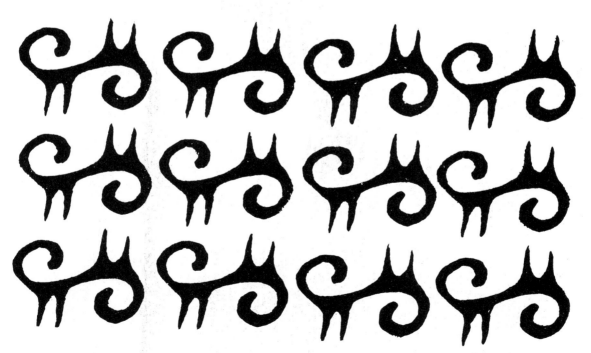

FIGURE 1–8
Ashanti, field manipulation.

PATTERN

FIGURE 1–9
Ashanti, field manipulation.

The linear motif, Figure 1-7, suggesting a fanciful animal with a long snout, or a thorny arabesque, or perhaps a dollar sign gone wrong, is from an African Ashanti printing stamp from Ghana. It possesses a naive charm coupled with considerable authority in its simple reverse symmetry. Figure 1-8 shows a standard method of using the shape—a straight row, space, another straight row, space, and so on—until the desired area is filled. Since the shape has an attractive if ambiguous figurative meaning and the white ground has none at all, attention is concentrated on the shape, or dark. However, in the curves of the snout-tail parts the light spaces can be seen as definite shapes with a character particularly their own, and the concept of "mutually defining dark-light" functions. But from row to subsequent row a light line appears, a thin horizontal stripe that contains no dark elements, and that visually seems lighter than the other light areas. This light stripe is a separation that weakens the all-over impression of the surface. By a simple shift, moving the rows closer together, as shown in Figure 1-9, the light areas make definite

FIGURE 1–10
Ashanti, field manipulation.

rounded joining shapes. It is possible to visually call up the white shapes as being of near equal importance to the darks.

Shifting the positions of the darks to that of an alternation, Figure 1-10, creates an entirely different emphasis in the reading: The surface loosens, becomes more curvilinear, and the horizontal banding of the rows is countered by subtle diagonal movements. The reverse curve of the figure becomes more emphatic and the thorn-like pairs of marks appended to them less important. By moving the rows closer together to minimize the amount of light, definite solid areas of light are created and read as shapes clearly combining with dark. The action and counteraction of dark-light become interdependent. They may not be equal to one another in amount or configuration, but they are equal in visual content and function in composing the surface.

DEVELOPING SHAPE SEQUENCES

Tracking a shape through variations while working with it is a rewarding way in which to build a large vocabulary of related shapes by learning to develop what the shape itself suggests. The ax-head (Figure 19 in the Introduction), varied by eliminating one of the small curved light areas, is used as a beginning for such a sequence, shown in Figure 1-11. The light bulge is enlarged, then relaxed to a quarter-circle, which in turn diminishes in amount as it pushes to the upper right hand corner of the grid unit, through the sequence. The dark areas correspondingly decrease and increase, and the sequence could as easily be started with dominant light as dominant dark. A new idea is introduced in the lower design units: Dark-light is shown not as two joined areas within the design

FIGURE 1–11
Ax-head variation sequence.

unit, but as three. The shape idea of the lower design unit could be sustained through another sequence, but there is enough material in the one shown to clearly demonstrate the idea of the method. There is need for imagination and free play in creating shapes—otherwise it is all dry bones. Once the creative juices have been primed by action as well as by reflection and start flowing, and attention has been taken away from the concern of making *a* shape, and thinking through connections instead, the process moves along and shapes develop almost spontaneously.

A summary sequence of patterns, in which the inner workings of proportionate amounts that effect the final surface reading can be studied, is shown in Figure 1-12. Four shapes from the examples in Figure 1-11 have been put in pattern statement on the grid,

FIGURE 1–12
Patterns based on Figure 1–11.

using a value reversal. The percentages of relative dark-light vary in each, consequently the surfaces appear quite different from one another although they are based on shapes taken from a closely related group. Using the experience from earlier series of shapes and patterns it is predictable that the two upper design units shown in Figure 1-11 will create stripes when aligned on the grid, and that the design unit shown last in the sequence will "spot out" or float, as indeed it does as shown in the pattern at the lower right of Figure 1-12.

The exchange of dark and light is best realized in the patterns at the upper and lower left of the illustration. In the first example, the dark-light shapes begin to fuse in a balance of proportionate amounts. The pattern has little else to recommend it, being somewhat banal in character. A sharp point created where the darks join in the repeat seems overly emphatic, calling too much attention to itself in contrast to the other softer, rounded elements of the surface, and calling up a stripe at the contrasting edge which partially negates the visual development of the curved element. The balance of dark-light in the pattern at the lower left is subtler, with angles and curves more evenly distributed for a better overall organization and containment of contrast. Here, too, there is not the obvious 50 percent dark and 50 percent light balance, which works successfully in many instances, but does not always have the interest that slightly more dark in relation to light, or more light to less dark, gives. The pattern shown at the upper right tends towards that loss of surface integration that has been seen when related amounts of dark-light in the design unit become too dissimilar in proportion, and the quarter circle begins to detach from the dark shape reducing it to the function of a ground rather than an equally interactive part of the entire surface. This effect is carried to the extreme in the pattern at the lower right, in which different proportionate amounts of shapes identical to those at its left are used. The darks are poorly defined, and the lights join in a complex shape, in high contrast to the dark, and read as small visual complications evenly spaced on the surface.

A PATTERN ANALYSIS

The pattern from a Bushongo raffia pile weave mat from the Republic of Zaïre (Figure 1-13) is a strong study in dark-light. The fretwork surface appears to

FIGURE 1–13
Bushongo raffia pile cloth pattern, Congo-Kinshana.
From *African Designs from Traditional Sources* by Geoffrey Williams.
© 1971 Dover Publications, Inc., New York.

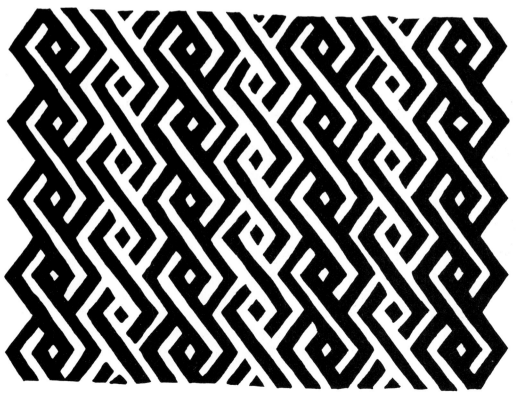

PATTERN

be very complex, but a close look reveals the simplicity of its organization: two bands of intertwined angles, one dominantly dark, the other light, join to form a single wide horizontal stripe. The dark-light balance is reversed from one half of the stripe to the other—easily seen if either the small light or dark diamond is thought of as the center of each of the bands, and the continuous zigzag line as the center of the entire stripe. This compound stripe is repeated along the length of the finished mat.

The motif of intertwining elements, or fretwork, is a common one appearing throughout the world in one stylistic version or another, and in fact, this example is but one of many variations used by the Bushongo for cloth patterning. It is a simple organization and its relation to the grid is diagrammed in Figure 1-14 as a repeat composed of two grid units arranged vertically.

This Bushongo pattern is a powerful example of dark-light interchange. There is no visual ambiguity in this surface. Every part is active in the composition of the whole: The amounts of dark and light are equal and interdependently defining. Although the pattern moves rapidly from left to right across the field, the composing elements are balanced and held within the pattern area. The long diagonal line is countered by shorter hook-like returns at top and bottom that make the intertwine, and the small central diamond shape is framed in such a way that it does not move but makes a series of centers in the bands. Both movements are subordinate to the dominant diagonal and keep the tensions of the surface in balance.

It is interesting to notice the differences between the top and bottom edges in the smaller section of the pattern shown in Figure 1-15. The top line is resolved in the light area framing the section, while the lower edge is aggressively contrasting to it and appears to move forward on the plane.

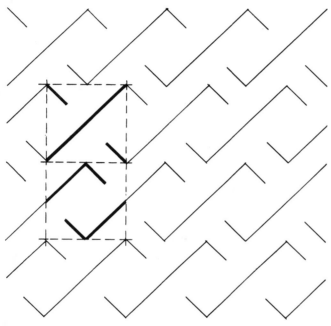

FIGURE 1–14
Diagram of Figure 1–13.

FIGURE 1–15
Edge detail of Figure 1–13.

GAME B

REVERSALS:
PLAYING WITH DARK-LIGHT COUNTERCHANGE

The ideas in every game played can be extended to discover new relationships and create new surfaces. Percentages stresses making shapes, dark-light, and how these relate to the grid and to surface structure. But Percentages is not all of pattern study. Design ideas are cumulative. Those already developed in one way may be continued or varied in new games.

   Reversals builds upon the previous game and can be played with the same shapes. The new idea is the old one of the checkerboard, or counterchange in dark and light in its simplest form—one square dark and one light, alternated in placement in succeeding rows, left to right, as shown in Figure 1-16. A more sophisticated use of reversing can be seen in Figure 1-13, in which the bands are alternately dark, then light, in turn. Although the bands are identical in design, the dark-light reversal gives each its particular character

and creates the strong articulation of the pattern when they are interlocked to complete the dark-light interchange.

FIRST MOVES

Any shapes from the previous sequences can be used to play Reversals. But to demonstrate that nothing is really lost, even though it may not succeed in its immediate context, two examples found to be weak when realized in pattern have been deliberately chosen to show the possibilities of transformation of the materials in this new framework. The first example is the smaller of the two angle shapes from Figure 1-5, which formed a stripe with a subordinate counterpoint angle in the upper right of the grid square, resulting in a surface on which the light area was so great—or the dark so small—that it lost identity as an interacting shape and became the ground for the dark figure. The second example, chosen to give contrast, is the curved shape shown in Figure 1-12, which has a better balance of dark-light, but gives an unresolved pattern configuration when joined with itself.

FIGURE 1–16
The checkerboard.

The first design unit is shown in Figure 1-17. When it is placed on the grid and each square in each row is reversed in dark-light without alternating the rows as in the checkerboard, a bold vertical stripe— shown on the left—is produced that is evenly balanced in its percentages of dark and light. When the placement is alternated, that is, a dominantly dark unit placed under a light one, the variation of a checkerboard shown on the right is produced—again, evenly balanced in dark-light proportions. It is interesting to compare the differences in pattern character revealed by these simple changes and study the contrast in scale between surfaces created from the original design unit and those which have been reversed, as well as the differences in character between stripe and checkerboard.

INCREASED REPEAT SIZE

When any set of design units is handled as a reversal the result will always be an equation of dark and light areas in the pattern, an even balance between them, and an immediate increase in the repeat size. This is because the areas are no longer complete within a single grid unit, but expand to two, joined side to side, when making a stripe, and four, when making a complete checkerboard unit since the alternation of position must be included in the repeat. In Reversals, emphasis again is placed not so much on what may appear to be an "interesting" design unit in itself, but on material to be worked through in different relationships.

The curved motif, or "C" shape, shown in Figure 1-18, has been given a quarter-turn clockwise within the grid unit to introduce the idea of a change of position as another method of gaining variety in the results of a thorough examination of a single design unit. Patterns are usually worked from one viewpoint, but any pattern should maintain a balance between its composing elements when turned and seen from different positions. Two patterns are produced using the methods described for the design shown in Figure 1-17. The results are those that would be expected, the difference being that the dominant movement of the surface on the left in Figure 1-18 is horizontal rather than vertical. The pattern on the right shows

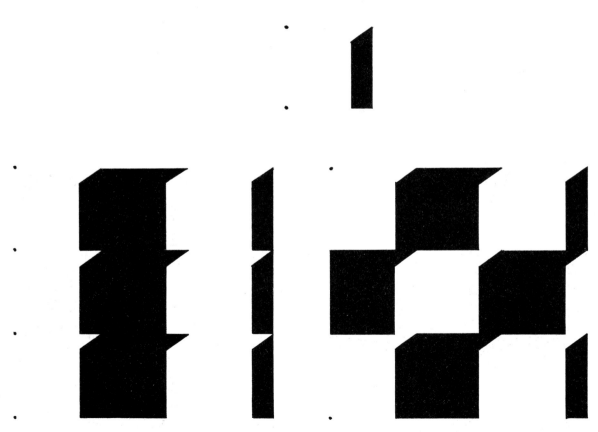

FIGURE 1–17
Small percent shape.

a more elaborate variation on a checkerboard than that seen in Figure 1-17. The small points abutting the straight line of the stripe seen in Figure 1-12 are resolved in both patterns as a continuous curvilinear flow against which the points contrast, but contrast within the context established by the pattern rather than as the contradiction to it seen in its previous use.

CHANGING SHAPE POSITIONS

As basic design units are transformed through the dark-light placement, the strengths and weaknesses of their potential surface movements are revealed. In addition to a vertical or horizontal movement, when a design unit is alternated row to row in dark-light, often a diagonal movement occurs in the pattern, such as that seen at the left in Figure 1-19. Although based on a very simple design unit taken from Figure 1-11, the continual interruption of the curve by the angle produces an unnecessary busyness at the line of dark-light contrast. The other pattern, shown at the right— based on another unit in the same series—eliminates

the angles and simplifies the dominant line of the pattern movement. Here, as in all of the preceding examples, critical comparison builds a foundation of experience upon which to make visual judgments, and emphasizes the importance of continuous work in shape development.

Three patterns, based on a design unit taken from Figure 1-2, are included in a final sequence of examples. Each one uses the foundation shown in Figure 1-20 to develop a surface. By following the methods used in the preceding illustrations the patterns shown in Figures 1-21 and 1-22 are produced. The first is a balanced surface with enough visual activity in its contained movements to make an interesting sharp-angled variation on a stripe. Composed of joined parallelograms, it reads equally well either vertically or horizontally. The alternation shown in Figure 1-22 is tentative and the dark-light line of contrast is poorly defined in comparison with the other examples. The long linear diagonal movement across the surface appears as structurally weak in relation to the planes and becomes all direction across the areas with little left *in* the surface.

FIGURE 1–18
Reversal shape.

PATTERN

FIGURE 1–19
Pattern comparison based on elements from Figure 1–11.

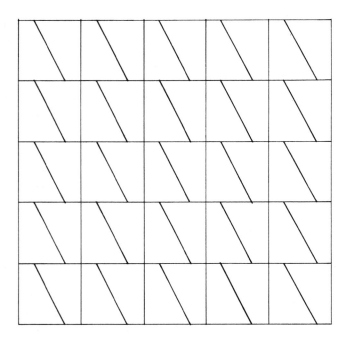

FIGURE 1–20
Reversal of Figure 1–2.

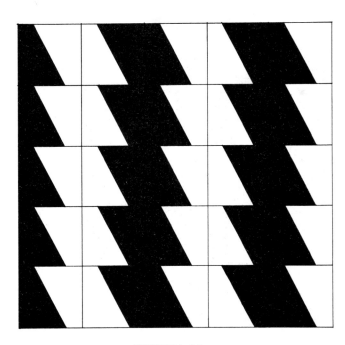

FIGURE 1–21
Reversal of Figure 1–2.

FIGURE 1–22
Reversal of Figure 1–2.

across the surface. This device gives a much tighter, more contained shape, preventing the ambiguous sprawl seen in Figure 1-22. The small right-angled articulations that appear where the design units join are completely integrated within the character of the design. The balance of the complete shape, which involves its equal—an idea similar to that of the African motif seen in Figure 1-7—and the diagonal movement on the surface is countered by the center of balance in the shape itself, giving a contained and clear surface reading to the pattern.

By comparing examples from Reversals with those of Percentages a shift in emphasis in relation to the grid can be seen. The grid was used as a right-angled control of the area in all of the work done in Percentages and is still used as such in Reversals. However, when shapes join to form new shapes, such as those in the lower right in Figures 1-18 and 1-23, much of the visual insistence of the grid framework diminishes in importance. It is still there as a static base, but curves, angles, horizontal, vertical, and diagonal movements become more dominant factors when reading the completed patterns.

Figure 1-23, the strongest pattern in the group, shows a reversal row by row down, rather than by grid unit to grid unit across. The second row is a dark-light reversal of the first, making a repeat that includes the upper and lower units; that, in turn, is repeated evenly

FIGURE 1–23
Reversal of Figure 1–2.

GAME C
MANIPULATIONS:
VARYING SHAPE PLACEMENT ON THE GRID

To manipulate a shape means to move it, to change its position. As position changes, new alignments and relationships are discovered, and when these relationships are repeated new patterns are formed. The Manipulations game is played by moving a single design unit—the basic dark-light combination—over the grid. Using the grid as a constant, and the design unit as a variable, the object of the game is to discover as many variations of the unit's position on the grid as possible. The design unit is placed in each grid unit in a certain way and repeated over the surface, or it is placed one way in one grid unit and another in the adjoining units, and this combination becomes the pattern repeat. Game A (Percentages) emphasized the porportionate relationship of dark-light balance in the design unit which was placed within the grid unit in a single position and repeated evenly over the surface to develop a pattern. There was no variation of position or placement of the design unit—it was always uniform. Game B (Reversals) continued the emphasis on dark-light balance in counterchange, or maintaining an equal balance from design unit to design unit by exchanging the placement of dark-light in adjoining design units, with the objective of keeping an equal balance of these elements on the surface.

Manipulations incorporates ideas from both games A and B, but places emphasis on variation of placement of the design unit within the grid units, and from unit to unit by rotating it, reversing it, or alternating its position. The result of playing Manipulations will be a series of contrasting patterned surfaces, all of which have been developed from the same visual elements, but with each showing different relationships between those elements. The important maneuver is one of changing—slightly or greatly—the relationship of position: it compounds shapes, creates new ones, and affects scale by increasing repeat size. These patterns are seen as the result of changing relationships, and although they may take forms such as checkerboard, stripe, half-drop, and so on, they do not evolve from working with predetermined or conventional pattern forms, but from working directly with the flat relations of the surface.

Another result is that the grid, so clearly stated as foundation in many patterns made while playing Percentages or Reversals, becomes subordinate to the pattern activity it supports. The diminution of the visual insistence of the grid structure was seen in Figures 1-18 and 1-19 in Game B, but as shapes are manipulated, and repeats become more complicated as a result, the grid disappears completely into the surface. When a half-dozen patterns are completed and viewed as a series, their resemblances in basic shape vocabulary, contrasted with their variety of repeat arrangements, clearly show a new emphasis on surface variety derived from working with a controlled distribution of shape relationships over the grid rather than using it as a contained structure with each cellular unit intact.

FIRST MOVES

Begin simply. As always, simplicity is stressed when designing an elementary design unit since complex or compound units are limited in the variety and number of their possible combination, and the connection between elements is certainly more important than the element itself in this game.

A right-angle triangle has been chosen to illustrate key moves in Manipulations. This familiar geometric shape when placed on the grid creates a design unit equal in dark-light balance. A one-to-one alignment over the surface produces the strong pattern structure shown in Figure 1-24. When two dark triangular shapes are placed in the same position in ad-

FIGURE 1–24
Pattern manipulation.

joining grid units the light interval between them becomes a complementary light triangle and the design unit is formed. When the third dark is positioned the relation of the design units clarifies and shows a complete interchange of equal dark and light, which is then repeated evenly across the surface. The pattern repeat is small scale, occupying only one grid unit. The shapes combine well because of their relative proportions and because the edge relation of the triangle is clear as it joins the grid outline on two sides, defining the complementary light triangle. The design unit does not give an imbalanced or disjointed effect which could result from overemphasizing either dark or light amounts or failing to relate the design unit to the edge of the grid unit. The pattern shown in Figure 1-24 is a straightforward use of the shape, giving a nicely proportioned surface that reads well when seen from any side. It is familiar as a foundation for many patterned surfaces that have been created from ancient to modern times.

ROTATIONS

In Figure 1-25 the configuration of the upper left grid unit is the same as that seen in Figure 1-24, but the grid unit immediately to the right of it shows the design unit rotated a quarter-turn in a clockwise direction,

FIGURE 1–25
Pattern manipulation.

FIGURE 1–26
Pattern manipulation.

which doubles the repeat size. This new unit is repeated evenly across the top and then placed in alternation to the position of the design units in the top row, in the second row down, which doubles the repeat size again, making it an area of four grid units. This arrangement is then repeated evenly over the surface. The pattern produced by these manipulations is larger in scale than the first, but equally strong in dark-light balance and reading. It, too, is another long used pattern structure.

In the third example, Figure 1-26, the dark triangle makes edge contact with the grid unit on its right and lower sides—the design unit has been rotated a quarter-turn counterclockwise from the original position. Another turn counterclockwise gives the second square to the right and, following the method used in Figure 1-25, this configuration is repeated across the top row. The second row, rather than being positioned in alternation to the first row, is shown as a reversal of it, increasing the repeat to four grid units in area, and this is repeated over the surface to give a pattern composed of counterbalanced parallelograms. There are subtle differences in this surface from those of the first two examples: it is strongly directional in character, which changes its reading when viewed from different positions, and the left and right edges change the entire effect of the pattern when it is given a half turn. There is a tendency for the edges

to detach from the body of the pattern and read—very slightly—as borders. This is an indication that the increase in repeat size, which results in an increase in the overall scale of the pattern, is becoming larger than the format can accomodate to maintain an integrated surface. This same effect can be seen in the right and left side triangles in Figure 1-25. They tend to be visually identified as separate units rather than being absorbed into a uniform surface distribution. If either pattern were to be increased in area the effect would diminish. Nevertheless, the pattern shown in Figure 1-26, with its contained countermotions is successful in its even balance of dynamic elements.

Figure 1-27 shows a pattern constructed with the same beginning move in the upper left grid unit as that shown in Figure 1-26. The design unit is flipped in mirror image in the adjoining unit to the right and the resultant design unit repeated in the top row. The second row is a dark-light reversal of the first, giving a large scale exchange of dark-light zigzag bars when repeated that can be read either vertically or horizontally. The grid foundation is taken over by the vigorous movement of dark and light on the surface.

Figure 1-28 is first cousin to Figures 1-26 and 1-27. The chevron is the same as that shown in Figure 1-27, and the method of reversal is that of Figure 1-26, but used with the symmetrical figure

FIGURE 1–27
Pattern manipulation.

FIGURE 1–28
Pattern manipulation.

intact rather than halved. Although the three patterns are closely related, each surface possesses characteristics unique to itself. They demonstrate the method of playing Manipulations: Move from simple positions of the design unit to more complex by carefully controlling the repeat size, its dark-light balance, and its alignment with itself. Again, the grid is the control for all moves made. Always bring forward and apply material from the earlier games, for that establishes a working frame of reference.

THE SCALE OF REPEATS

Repeats should not become too large or overly complicated; they must be in scale with the area being covered or the sense of rhythm, essential in good pattern, will be lost. At least three full repeats across and down the surface should be shown so the relationship and the rhythm of their order is clear. With fewer repeats no sense of cumulative rhythm can be seen.

Figure 1-29 continues the idea shown in Figure 1-27, but with a dramatic increase in scale. It is a logical continuation of the design theme, but has outgrown the area available for its realization. An increase in the area—making it much larger in overall size—would solve the problem. The position of the dark-light design unit in the upper left corner is the same

FIGURE 1–29
Pattern manipulation.

as that of the three preceding patterns; the second unit in the top row is a mirror image of the first, or a quarter rotation clockwise; the third unit is a reversal of the second, or a half-rotation counterclockwise; and the fourth a mirror image of the third, or a quarter rotation counterclockwise within the grid unit. The repeat is completed in the second row where the four design units reading from the left margin are shown as dark-light reversals of those in the top row. The pattern is made with a regular alignment of this eight unit repeat. Given a total grid area of eight by eight grid units, four full repeats can be shown going down the area, but only two across, thereby resulting in a crowded surface that is visually uncomfortable. The pattern demands more area—a large scale format—for full realization. The top and bottom edges show the same problem seen in previous examples: the two dark triangles at the top detach, and the entire line of the bottom appears as though made up of separate elements. Again, an increase in size would resolve the edges. This condition of edges detaching from the pattern area is a common one, and occurs again and again when working on a small format. But it is more important to create many examples of pattern manipulation and compare them in series than it is to make one or two very large examples that take as much time to finish as it would to make half a dozen smaller ones that give the same essential visual information.

The pattern shown in Figure 1-30 should be com-pared to that shown in Figure 1-26 since both use an identical shape with a contrasting result. The first move—the position of the design unit in the upper left corner of the grid—returns to that of Figure 1-24. The second design unit is a dark-light reversal of it, making a full repeat which gives a lively but balanced surface.

ALTERNATIONS

The same design unit used in Figure 1-30 is used in Figure 1-31, but it is reversed in the second row, or alternated in position. That is, the second square in the repeat developed in the first row becomes the first square of the second row in an alternation—or, it can be looked at as a reversal of the design unit in the upper left corner of the grid. The pattern is large in scale but so simple in organization that it holds well on the surface. It is interesting to compare this pattern with the one shown in Figure 1-24. There, the surface fluctuates between dark-light squares, diagonal movements, and right angles in dark and light, all equally balanced to give a nearly static reading when compared to the dramatic diagonal thrust of the surface shown in Figure 1-31. Yet each pattern contains exactly the same percentage of dark and light in the design unit and also in the finished surface. The first reflects the grid foundation; the second annihilates it.

FIGURE 1–30
Pattern manipulation.

FIGURE 1–31
Pattern manipulation.

Essentially, the top row of Figure 1-32 reflects the organization of the top row of Figure 1-29, although the first move is that of the first pattern shown in the position of the design unit in the upper left corner of the grid. But primarily, this is an example of the effect of alternation of rows. If the grid units are numbered 1, 2, 3, 4, from upper left across in the top row, then in the second row 2 becomes 1, and 3 becomes 2; in the third row 3 becomes 1, and 4 becomes 2; and in the fourth row down 4 becomes 1, and so on. This is less complicated in practice than it reads, and gives a completely new pattern result.

The repeat is composed of sixteen grid units. Such a size can become unwieldly unless it is thought of as being built of carefully controlled single units combined in a planned alternated arrangement. Although the size of the repeat is large for the total area shown, the proportion of elements is small enough to give a good idea of the pattern, but the full effect of the diagonal cannot be seen until the total pattern area is increased in size.

COMBINING ROTATIONS AND ALTERNATIONS

The pattern shown in Figure 1-33 is developed by rotating the position of the design unit and then alternating its position from row to row. The dark-light triangles are turned clockwise, or rotated a quarter-

FIGURE 1–32
Pattern manipulation.

FIGURE 1–33
Pattern manipulation.

turn in each of the four squares beginning in the upper left grid unit and moving to the right. The row is then placed in alternation in the second row down, the second unit of the first row now becomes the first unit in the second row, making a full repeat of eight grid units. An active surface, full of movements and countermovements, is the result. It can be read as a combination of diamonds, turnings in the small triangles, and cross diagonals, with all the elements in equilibrium.

The same design unit is based in Figure 1-34, but the alternation is carried down four rows rather than two, which is the same method used to develop the surface shown in Figure 1-32. The pattern is simpler in organization, and clearer in its overall effect, than that of Figure 1-33. Although it does not have as much variety of content as that pattern, it is a better integrated surface, depending only upon cross diagonals in contrasting scales for its effect. Both patterns can be given a half-turn to change the surface character by having the small triangles point down rather than up, in much the same way that relative position affects the reading of almost any pattern except that of the completely static checkerboard.

The sequence of eleven patterned surfaces demonstrates some possibilities of playing Manipulations. The game may be continued with still more variations with the basic elements of grid and shape, additional patterns created using the dark-light triangle design unit, or a new series started with a unit different in

FIGURE 1–34
Pattern manipulation.

its percentage balance of dark and light, or one curvilinear rather than angular in outline. Each example uses exactly the same design vocabulary, the same proportionate amounts of dark and light, the same size grid unit, yet each is distinctly different from the other in its finished surface effect because of the continually changing relationship of the pattern components, not the components themselves.

Manipulations should be played as a progression from a simple unit placed on the grid, combined with itself, then varied, increasing in pattern complexity through a series of examples. Rather than concentrating on the limitation of creating a single pattern, it should be played as a continuum of expanding relationships, from simple to complex, between the common design elements, and should utilize the work done in Percentages and Reversals to increase the pattern making possibilities.

GAME D
VISUAL GRAY:
DEPTH IN THE PATTERN PLANE

Up to this point pattern surfaces have been defined by the single contrast of dark and light. The function of each value has been not to support but to exchange with the other, as all elements of the surface structure are utilized as being visually equal in importance. This balance of contrasts is easier to achieve when the percentage of dark is equal to that of light, but—as examples have shown—careful proportioning of unequal amounts of dark-light in the design unit can produce integrated surfaces. The basic parts of all patterns, simple or complex, have been the same: a grid, a shape, a design unit, a repeat. The interplay of these components has been developed as pattern through dark-light contrast on the surface. In a successful interchange, dark and light remain in the same plane:

FIGURE 1–35
Kata-gami: Bush Clover and Sky. 20 × 35.3 cm.
Courtesy of Cooper-Hewitt Museum, The Smithsonian Institution's National Museum of Design.

One does not recede or advance in relation to the other on the surface. A third value establishes a planar relationship *within* the surface, such as that shown in Figure 1-35. Dark and light are extremes of contrast; between them a series of grays can be placed that move incrementally from darker to lighter, centering on a middle value.

Visual gray is a continuation of the study of pattern construction in dark-light interchange. Parts of the pattern repeat are handled in such a way that they appear as mid-value in relation to adjacent dark and light areas. For example, in Figure 1-36, the lines of contrast between dark and middle, and middle and light, appear equal in definition. The mid-value is not an actual solid gray of paper pasted on the surface, or painted in from a mixture of black and white pigment, but an illusion of gray produced by the regular spacing of small amounts of black and white which mix in the eye and read as gray when compared to black and white. The size of the lines or dots that compose the gray is critical, for if they are too large and read as separate elements rather than merging when viewed from distance or seen through a reducing glass, the effect is lost.

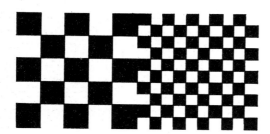

FIGURE 1–36
Three-step visual gray value scale.

A visual gray manipulation of a different sort is shown in Figure 1-37. This is a legitimate design tool that increases the possibilities of pattern making not by adding an irrelevant embellishment to the existing pattern, but by incorporation into the structure of a

FIGURE 1–37
Visual gray checkerboard.

functioning part in the total surface reading. Nor is this a figure-field relationship. Rather, it establishes an exchange of position on and within the surface plane which must be held in balance with other composing elements. It is simpler to use a solid gray, but a visual gray is an economic move which takes the materials at hand to develop new design elements, expand their use, and make more of them. Visual gray is not achieved by adding a new element *to* the surface; it is drawn *out* of the surface, thereby giving it depth and textural interest.

VISUAL GRAY
IN JAPANESE STENCILS

In their variety and design inventiveness old Japanese stencils are unrivalled as a source of dark-light study. Three have been chosen to show how a visual gray can be used to create value gradations, to soften the edges of shapes, and to change the relative positions of planes in the surface. The first example, Figure 1-38, illustrates a range of mid-value densities made up by spacing lines at different distances apart. Although the shapes formed by the placement of the plume-like figure are not consistently clear, the overall design is a graceful surface developed by using only straight and curved lines. The shapes are distributed asymmetrically over a ground of evenly spaced fine lines that reads as a uniform mid-value. The different thicknesses of some of the curved lines is not as interesting a structural idea as that of the many value gradations that occur when lines of an even thickness are placed at varying distances from each other, and subtler fluctuations of dark and light happen, punctuated by the small flower-shaped dots of dark. If a consistent line width had been used in the entire design, or a thick line for the supporting gray, and a slightly thicker but uniform line for the other shapes—and a clearer definition had been given to the interplay between those shapes—a better balance of elements could have been achieved.

Although the surface illustrated diverges from the main concerns of integrated pattern, it is an excellent example of a sophisticated use of a single element—line—to create a series of visual grays, and should be studied in relation to the diagrams shown in Figures 1-36 and 1-37, to understand better the importance of scale and amount, and the manner in which the dark-light divisions must be juxtaposed to give a visual reading of gray.

In the second example, Figure 1-39, a rippling movement developed in dark-light shape interchange is shown. This is a free interpretation of a checker-

GAME D: VISUAL GRAY

board pattern structure. Each unit is bonded to the other at top and bottom with a serrate edge of visual gray, which is in keeping with the diffuse character of the surface.

The final example, Figure 1-40, is based on a combination of stylized motifs that are separated and boxed into a sturdy grid. The grid would seem disproportionate to the other design elements if it were not for the pairs of white crosses placed on it that reduce its weight. The high contrast squares containing double bars enclosing a square of gray are positioned on a surface that appears to be above that of the mid-value lattice-figured squares. Although there are two uses of visual gray, that of the lattice pattern and the small square centered within the bars, the latter remains firmly in the plane of its surrounding dark. It reads as a gray darker than that of the lattice which moves it towards the dark rather than the light values. From a distance the heavy border surrounding the alternated units seems to join the higher value contrasts of the double bar unit, enlarging it and pushing the mid-value still further back in its planar position.

The three examples should be seen as a sequence of means of making and using visual gray, and related

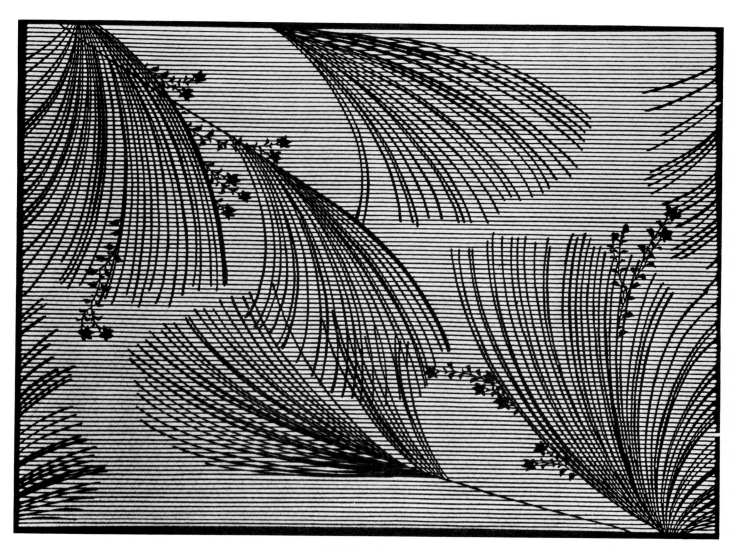

FIGURE 1–38
Kata-gami: Straw Grass.
Courtesy of The Seattle Art Museum, Eugene Fuller Memorial Collection.

FIGURE 1–39
Kata-gami: Geometric Pattern Imitating Flame Stitch. 19.4 × 35 cm.
Courtesy of Cooper-Hewitt Museum,
The Smithsonian Institution's National Museum of Design.

to the patterns that have been made by playing the games. The first (Figure 1-38) shows an asymmetrical composition of linear elements; the second (Figure 1-39) a very broad interpretation of a checkerboard; and the third (Figure 1-40) a symmetrical pattern, again based on a checkerboard. The direct relation is in the variety of grays produced using different amounts of dark and light. Keep in mind that the stencils are single repeats of a total design and are meant to be joined at the edges when printed on a length of cloth. Other characteristics of the patterns would appear when they are used that way. The curved diagonal movement, which is not obvious in the first stencil, would be emphasized when the design was repeated, as would the nearly invisible diagonal movement of the small elements in the second. The disproportionate size of the units for the repeat area, in the third stencil, would disappear and the dark-light

reading of the larger unit would become stronger, causing the gray unit to recede even further into the surface.

FIRST MOVES

Figure 1-41 shows some possible combinations of values made using the design unit from Figures 1-24 through 1-34. They are combinations of thick and thin lines placed to produce an illusion of gray. Hatching, stippling, or combinations of elements can be used, depending upon the effect desired and whether it seems appropriate for the finished pattern. There are many ways of making visual grays that can be used in constructing new pattern readings, as an hour spent with some graph paper and one or two felt-tipped pens will readily show. To demonstrate only some of the many variations possible, four design units have been

40

FIGURE 1–40
Kata-gami: Hemp Leaf and Well-cover Motifs. 14 × 34.7 cm.
Courtesy of Cooper-Hewitt Museum,
The Smithsonian Institution's National Museum of Design.

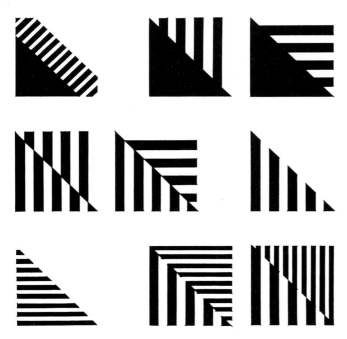

FIGURE 1–41
Visual gray triangle shape manipulation.

FIGURE 1–42
Triangle with crenelated edge.

chosen from Figure 1-41 and used on patterns made playing Manipulations (Figures 1-24, 1-26, 1-31 and 1-33). Any of these variations, or others, can be used as a basis to rethink patterns made in Percentages and Reversals.

A crenelated edge is used to join the dark-light triangles in the design unit shown in Figure 1-42. Diagonal lines, always suggesting a strong counter-action in relation to a right-angled format, are implicit in the original pattern, and the gray line emphasizes that movement. The line establishes its visual position as raised slightly from the pattern surface, and its effect is to soften the high dark-light contrast. There is little change in the relative proportion of values, gray being in definite subordination to dark and light, and there is no change in repeat size. Since a new move-

41

ment is formed in visual gray that changes the character of the pattern, the gray edge cannot be considered an embellishment, but an integral and functioning part of the new surface. However, it does not affect the basic pattern construction, which remains identical to that of the model upon which it is based—a spare, simple surface, as effective in dark-light as its variation using visual gray.

RE-INTERPRETING DARK-LIGHT PATTERNS

If a dark-light unit is translated to a dark-middle balance, the reading of the new surface will be as different from the original as the mid-value is from the extreme value contrast; the same is true for a light-middle value relationship. Although the value shift will cause a definite change in the final surface effect, there will be no change in the surface structure. There is a change in character from the original pattern shown in Figure 1-42, and Figure 1-43 (based on Figure 1-26) shows a change in surface effect but no change in pattern reading. Both examples are of exactly the same construction as that of their original models. In Figure 1-44, however, two mid-values are used—one darker, one lighter by comparison—which enlarges the repeat size, and a stripe is drawn out of the surface by alternate placement of the value contrasts. Here the struc-

ture of the surface varies from the original, and that variation causes the change in the surface effect.

Using three values makes it possible to emphasize one or the other. Either dark, middle, or light can dominate in amount and the proportionate relationships of dark-light will have to be redistributed if a pattern, previously designed with one value contrast, is being used as a basis. For example, the pattern on the left in Figure 1-45 shows a new balance in the strong diagonal bars. Drawn from the pattern shown in Figure 1-31, the repeat has doubled in size to accommodate the placement of gray in the design unit; there is twice as much dark used as either middle or light. An interesting variation on the same pattern is shown at the right, in which the same proportions of value are observed as in the example on the left, but the repeat is reduced to four units across making a contrasting saw-tooth stripe running parallel to the dominant dark. Both patterns show an increase in visual interest from that of the model pattern for the same reasons observed in the preceding examples: textural variations in the gray areas, planar variations within the surface, and the discovery of contrasting countermovements uncovered by value manipulation.

However, in all the examples, visual gray has been included in strict adherence to the organization of a pre-existing pattern. Surface characteristics have been re-formed, with care taken that the gray functions as part of those characteristics, not as a deco-

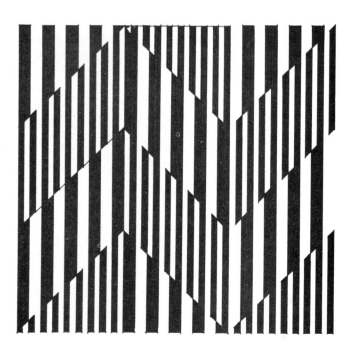

FIGURE 1–43
Pattern reinterpretation in visual gray.

FIGURE 1–44
Pattern reinterpretation in visual gray.

GAME D: VISUAL GRAY

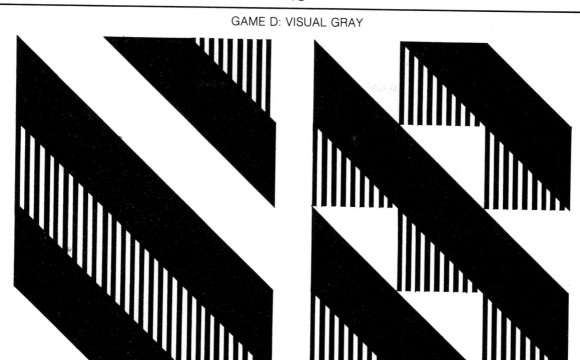

FIGURE 1–45
Pattern reinterpretation in visual gray.

ration. But there has not been a full manipulation of the surface in a series of grays developed *from* the model—rather, they have been based *upon* the model.

A different approach is taken to develop the surface shown in Figure 1-46. A uniform line density covers the entire pattern area with an even gray tonality. Using contrasting line densities and cross-hatching, a design unit is created with a series of values which is repeated evenly across the grid, then alternated in placement in the second row down, following the construction of the original diagonal stripe pattern. Although the design unit and repeat position are identical with those of the model pattern, the surface has actually been re-created with equal movements of value contrast related in a sequence.

Figures 1-45 and 1-46 should be compared to see the relative plane positions in the surface made possible by more than one value contrast. The elements in the pattern on the left in Figure 1-45 tend to remain in the same plane. The gray stripe joins the dark diagonals, increasing the pattern scale and emphasizing the strong diagonal movement. The light stripe gains in visual importance because of the contrast in proportionate amounts of light and middle and dark. The slight fluctuation of the surface depth in the gray stripe is flattened by the high contrast of the light value and all the areas remain in a balanced exchange in a single plane.

The same proportionate amounts of light and middle value are distributed in a different manner in the pattern on the right in Figure 1-45, and the sawtooth diagonal stripe moves into the surface plane with dark bars cutting across the top of it. A further condition affecting the planar differences is the sharp contrast of the light and middle value triangles. Rather than a smooth single movement, a subordinate right angle is introduced, a contrast that emphasizes not only the difference in value, but also the difference of a direct diagonal motion contrasted with the hesitation of a stepped motion. Both value contrast and the shape and position of the contrasting area will cause a change in relative surface depths. Another example of this effect can be seen in the Japanese stencil shown in Figure 1-35.

Parallel lines and cross-hatching create the succession of advancing and receding planes in four values shown in Figure 1-46. The diagonal movement of the original pattern is maintained by grouping the pair of darker values in one stripe and the lighter values in the other. Further emphasis is given to the movement by the line of high contrast between the lightest and the darkest values in every other diagonal stripe. The saw-tooth edge stripe from Figure 1-45, right, is maintained, but used in a different and more effective way. It creates a subordinate sub-movement in the surface that is integrated into the entire pattern sur-

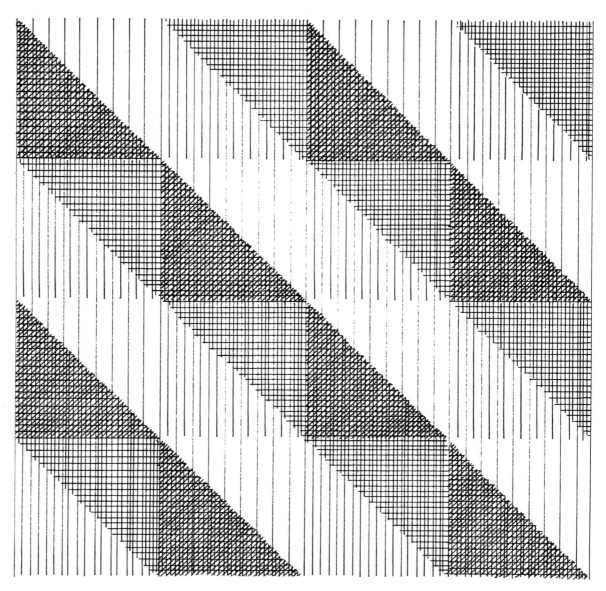

FIGURE 1–46
Pattern reinterpretation in visual gray.

face rather than depending upon contrast alone for its effect. The value sequence moves from light to middle, to middle-dark, to dark, corresponding to the organization of the stripes in the original pattern. The stripes, rather than being side by side, appear to be moving over and under each other, and the step motion becomes part of each. The diagonal movements combine in a visual counterpoint bonded by the value sequence into a surface contained and complete in its organization, and richer in visual reading than either of the preceding examples.

Simple pattern structures, such as the dark-light triangle design unit, and the diagonal stripe, are the best choices for foundation work in developing and using visual gray, just as a simple shape is best for beginning work in pattern. The sequence of examples

shown throughout Manipulations demonstrates how quickly relationships between simple design elements compound themselves when using only a dark-light contrast. Visual gray is a new—and further compounding—design material that can transform existing pattern structure, making a surface that differs little or completely from that upon which it is based; it connects with its model, but makes possible effects not obtainable with the single contrast of dark-light. How it is developed is a continuation of what is already in a given surface, not as extraneous ornamentation such as that of a florid vocal style, in which the singer's trills and leaps may thrill the listener, but frequently have little to do with the continuity of musical line, and attention is diverted from the song and put on the physical act of singing it. Depth in the surface is not making holes in it; it is constructed with the same attention to the overall surface consistency as a pattern made from dark-light contrast alone. The differences are as subtle as those of a musical *rubato*; the tempo of the visual action on the surface differs from the regular beat of a single dark-light contrast and emphasis is given to the in-out pulse of areas stressed and released as they relate to the uniform rhythmic movement over the area.

Although visual gray may be used in its own right to make new patterns without reference to present models, beginning moves stress evolving a visual gray from existing dark-light material and using it with existing pattern forms to study its effect on surface structure by comparison with known examples. Familiarity with the possibilities of visual gray comes from working with it and analyzing results. Patterns already established give the necessary comparative frame of reference, showing to what degree a pattern may be altered in structure with the appropriate or inappropriate use of the new design material. Comparison makes it apparent that certain surfaces are so complex in organization, large in scale, or appear so complete in themselves, that they stand as finished dark-light patterns and should be left as such without extending their forms further by reworking them to include a gray. Others—usually the simpler organizations—stand not only as finished patterns, but make excellent bases for new patterns including three or four values. The diagonal stripe is just such a pattern. It is impos-

sible to decide what makes a suitable pattern base for an extension, and what does not, until some work has been done, and the results given a thorough critical analysis based on the design experiences of Percentages, Reversals, and Manipulations.

POSSIBLE WRONG MOVES

A value manipulation that may work well with one pattern form may be unsuccessful when used with a different form. What is successful on a simple structure may fail when applied to one more complex. For example, Figures 1-47 and 1-48 are based on the pattern shown in Figure 1-33, which is complicated in its rotations and counteractions of diagonals and stripes composed of alternating triangles. By expanding the dark-light range to four values and grouping the darks in one grid unit and the lights in the adjoining unit, then alternating their positions in successive rows—the same alternation as that used in the original—a checkerboard is drawn out of the surface making a strong static field which absorbs some of the complexity of the original and simplifies the general effect of the pattern. However, piling up effects does little to create a wholly integrated surface. The pattern used as a model is not strong in organization: It lacks a clear rhythm and a dominant movement. The design unit is simple, and dark and light are proportionately

FIGURE 1–47
Pattern reinterpretation in visual gray.

FIGURE 1–48
Pattern reinterpretation in visual gray.

PATTERN

balanced, but the accumulation of activity on the surface is not supported by an intelligible basic structure. Attempting to make a checkerboard out of it does give a different emphasis to the organization, which subordinates much of the original pattern and makes an interesting contrast to it; but it appears as more of a remedial action than a new surface. It does not deal with the materials of the model in the manner of the examples shown in Figure 1-46, in which the original dark-light structure has been recast exactly, but varied subtly with value to gain greater surface depth. Rather, it attempts to change an original structure which was confused because it included too much, and the checkerboard is more camouflage than construction.

Figure 1-48 subordinates the checkerboard by a method similar to that used in the right-hand surface in Figure 1-45. Since the dark assumes the greater percentage of the area—and is an exact transcription of the placement of dark in the original pattern—there is very little change in the surface reading. However, if the original pattern reads as containing too much activity, there is hardly a point in adding another visual element, a sub-checkerboard of gray, to an already overloaded surface.

The pattern shown in Figure 1-49 maintains the original dark-light shape positions, but each triangle carries a wide edge of contrasting value, a variation of the idea used in Figure 1-42. As a result, another pattern is drawn out of the surface: a diamond emphasized by the edge of light value. This new configuration is out of relationship with the original pattern, and rather than amplifying the structure through the

FIGURE 1–49
Pattern reinterpretation in visual gray.

use of value gradation it adds an element in the diamond pattern that is not only unnecessary but confusing, since one kind of pattern is carried by the placement of the darks and another by the light values, minimizing the function of both grays.

In the first example, Figure 1-47, the original pattern has been reduced to a decorative ground since it has little direct connection to the dominant checkerboard pattern; the second, Figure 1-48, shows a reversal of emphasis with the now subordinate checkerboard adding an unnecessary sub-pattern; and, in the third, Figure 1-49, the original pattern is put into conflict with a new, superimposed pattern. The model pattern was developed by rotating the design unit on the grid, adhering to the simple moves necessary; in Figure 1-49, a new pattern form, that of the diamond, emerges. Both are complete forms in themselves. The example shown in Figure 1-47 has the advantage of the simplicity of the checkerboard form—whether it has anything to do with the original pattern or not—and could be developed as a visual theme in its own right; the third example, however, adds complication to complication, and fails because the basis of the surface becomes completely muddled in a variety of unrelated effects. What has to be handled is the material implicit in the original pattern.

What could be done with the original pattern in value sequence development? Very little, if anything. If a pattern becomes complicated through a series of simple moves, as has been shown over and over in the preceding examples; when a conclusion is arrived at (such as the pattern in Figure 1-33) it must be considered finished at that point. The simplicity of the diagonal pattern of Figure 1-31 allows for further development; the complexity of Figure 1-33 does not.

CREATING PATTERNS WITH VISUAL GRAY

It is not enough to add some value variation to a pattern successfully realized in the single contrast of dark-light only. Unless the surface is transformed—is changed in its reading—by the new manipulation, there is little point in doing it. Veneering the surface with textural interest in a value sequence adds nothing to that surface but visually empty decoration devoid of any structural meaning. The purpose of using visual grays to increase dimension within the surface does not differ from the purpose of careful control of proportionate dark and light in the design unit: to create an integrated pattern surface; but it is a new material, with its own characteristics, and has to be handled as such. For example, the patterns shown in Figures

1-50, 1-51, and 1-52 are based on the first pattern developed in Manipulations—the simple form of the evenly repeated dark-light triangles.

The first pattern, Figure 1-50, uses an even gradation of value from dark to light, with equal amounts of dark and light in the same positions as those of the original design unit, but with a joining edge of middle values—again, equal to each other in amount. The form remains the same as the model, but the characteristics of the new pattern are quite different from it since the shift from a bold dark-light contrast to value sequence softens the surface and creates a depth in it that does not exist in the original.

The same pattern base is used in Figure 1-51, but the dark-light disposition has been broken into bars that are alternated in their position in the design unit—a device taken from the series of visual gray manipulations shown in Figure 1-41. The alignment follows that of the original, but the resultant configuration is independent from the model, a surface unique in itself composed of linear diagonal movements running over the solid bars of the secondary plane.

Figure 1-52 continues the use of breaking areas into grays using parallel bands of dark and light, but adheres to the position of the dark and light triangles of the model by changing the scale of the bars, and consequently changing their relative value reading.

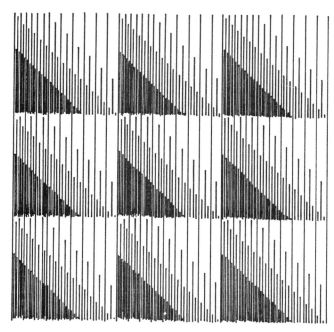

FIGURE 1-50
Pattern reinterpretation in visual gray.

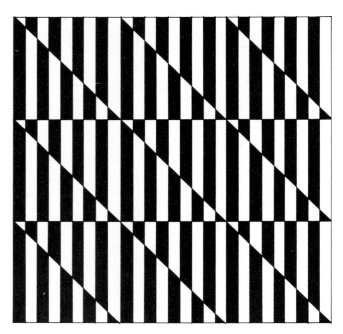

FIGURE 1–51
Pattern reinterpretation in visual gray.

FIGURE 1–52
Pattern reinterpretation in visual gray.

By opposing the position of the bars distinct triangular shapes are created. It is another design unit taken from Figure 1-41. Here again, the rhythm does not deviate from the one-to-one beat of the original, but reads apart from it. One moment it appears as a regular massing of uniform squares, the next as advancing dominant triangles against subordinate receding triangles.

All three surfaces have a common pattern base, but each is as different in its reading from the other as it is different from the original. The first, Figure 1-50, adheres more closely to the original pattern form than do the other two. It depends upon a simply value gradation to introduce a subtle diagonal movement across the surface and an in-out pulse within the surface. The patterns shown in Figure 1-51 and 1-52, on the other hand, contrast to the model in their use of visual grays as the raw material of the design and the surfaces are developed entirely with them.

The method is to use the framework of the basic pattern, rather than the pattern itself. That is, the design unit and its alignment on the grid is a reflection of the original model, but the exact disposition of dark-light is not re-created. In Figure 1-51, the design unit from Figure 1-41 is used, and it is used in exactly the same manner that the dark-light design unit was used in the original. It is the structure of the model pattern that is observed, not its particulars of development in

dark-light. For elementary patterns the process seems a simple one, but it is the same process that can be used when re-interpreting more complex patterns than the ones used in the examples.

Visual gray can easily become a study in itself. From the few simple maneuvers shown its possibilities can be extended to amplify nearly all of the work done to this point. The methods of creating visual gray vary from the example of a cautious development of the edge shown in Figure 1-42 to the complete re-interpretation of a surface shown in Figure 1-52. The criterion is that visual gray be evolved from the pattern structure itself rather than being applied to it in a disruptive or irrelevant way. Visual gray will not only give new patterns from old pattern forms, but entirely new patterns with their own forms.

A PATTERN STRUCTURE ANALYSIS

A detail of a large cloth from the Baule tribal group in Africa is shown in Figure 1-53. The entire cloth measures 1.6 meters wide by 2.75 meters long, and is fabricated by sewing together bands of woven material approximately 9 centimeters wide. Before threading the loom and weaving each band, the cotton yarn used as a warp is prepared by being tied in bundles of a predetermined length, with some areas exposed and

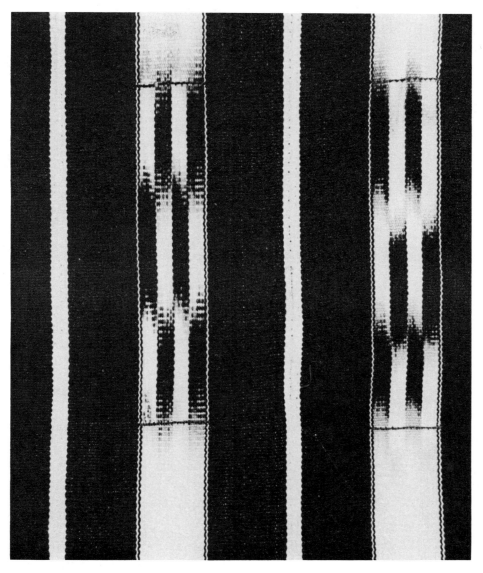

FIGURE 1–53
Baule cloth, detail.

some areas reserved with a tight binding. The yarn is then dipped into a dye vat until the desired depth of color is obtained; then it is rinsed and dried. The exposed areas of yarn become dyed, but the areas which were reserved by tieing remain the original color of the yarn. By careful calculation before the dye process is begun, a design can be planned on the basis of what parts will be left undyed and what parts will be dyed. The loom is warped with the threads and the bands are woven off, then sewn together to make a fabric of the desired width. The bands, or strips of cloth manufactured on a rudimentary loom by the weaver, are of the plain "tabby" weave—a balanced weave on the over-one, under-one method. The finished piece is actually a fabrication of units: narrow strips combined into a large cloth which carries a minor embellishment of supplementary embroidery.

The simplest materials: strands of cotton yarn, a dye vat, and an unsophisticated but effective loom are all that are used to make the component parts of the pattern—the design units. These are then arranged in a sequence to make the whole cloth (Figure 1-54). Each band is first bordered by a thin white selvage. The center stripe contains equally spaced rectangles of light and dark-light visual gray framed on either side by bold dark stripes. When one band is

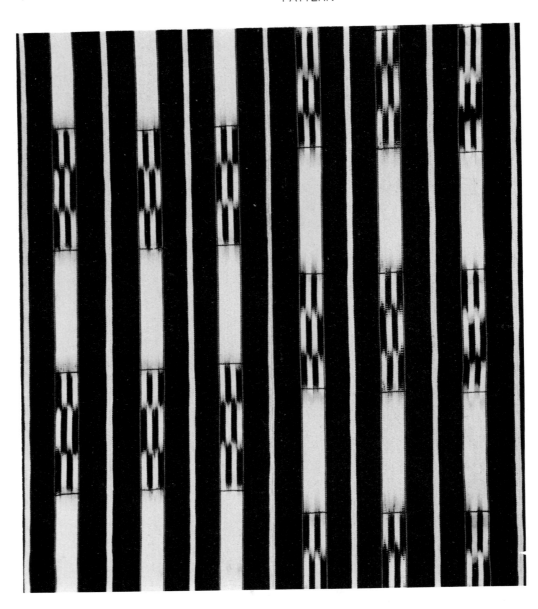

FIGURE 1–54
Baule cloth, section.

attached to another band the selvages form a narrow light line centered on a dominant dark stripe. The bands are then arranged in groups of three making a large-scale compound stripe. The adjoining group of three is alternated in placement by nearly a full unit drop, then the next group is returned to the original position. Throughout this manipulation the dominant dark stripe remains stationary across the surface while the lighter values re-group in a checkerboard of horizontal rectangles, making a counterpoint sub-pattern which appears to be positioned below the plane of the stripes. Another pattern could be made by alternating the design units in every other row, rather than by grouping them in threes, to make a small scale check-erboard; or, the design units could be put together in alternation to make a counterstripe running horizontally across the surface. But the surface of the full cloth as realized, shown in Figure 1-55, remains the most interesting of the possibilities in its union of contrasts.

The complete pattern is a fusion of two pattern forms—the stripe and the checkerboard—carefully balanced in their porportionate relationship. Both forms are implicit in the design unit, but must be realized by manipulating the unit. The combination does not cause a clash, but an amalgamation of the two forms in which their opposing rhythms create an exciting visual tension. The dark stripe clearly domi-

FIGURE 1–55
Baule cloth, full.

nates the surface in amount—there is nearly four times the amount of dark to either light or middle value—and in place, as it stands forward from the plane of the checkerboard. This position is further emphasized by the contrast in size between the heavier stripe and the smaller elements in lighter values which visually place the checkerboard on a secondary surface plane. The checkerboard of flattened rectangles, though subordinate in position and less emphatic in control, maintains its identity in the interchange with the controlling structure of the surface, which is the stripe. It establishes the scale, the rhythm, and the major vertical movement in the completed pattern.

GAME E
SCALE-CHANGE:
MANIPULATING THE GRID

In the Baule cloth we saw the effective use of dark-light, manipulation, and visual gray—all familiar parts of pattern making—in combination with variety in scale—large elements contrasting with small elements—and with a controlled combination of contrasting pattern forms. Developing new patterns and combinations of patterns as a result of manipulations has been discussed in Games C and D and is not a new phenomenon. But the idea of using various scales, or related sizes, to manipulate proportionate amounts in area from large to small, is new.

Scale-change is played with contrasts of large and small areas in repetition. Percentages and Manipulations, and their extensions, depend upon the control of a fixed foundation grid to structure a consistent surface. Just as it is possible to manipulate design units over the grid, so it is possible to manipulate the grid itself to produce variations in size and contrasts in emphasis that will give a richness and variety to the pattern result not obtainable by repeating units of the same size. Scale-change means changing the scale of the pattern within the pattern. The pattern unit does not change; it remains constant. The grid unit changes.

The design question is how to change and hold the change in context; how to establish contrasts of large and small and move them over the surface with seeming freedom to produce the enrichment and ten-sion of contrast without losing direction and creating a surface full of spots and holes that would destroy the inherent evenness of pattern. The answer is that changes must be made in accord with an established measure and that the design units must move in ratio and rhythm to that measure or there will be no control and pattern realization will be lost. Control is still in the grid since how it is used creates the modulation in scale. As a pattern unit can be manipulated over a grid by changing its position within the grid unit, so the pattern can be used as a static over a grid that has been manipulated through a sequence of changes in related sizes. Emphasis is put on the manner of the change which must take place within the repetitive mode to maintain pattern form. The transition from one point to a contrasting point is the design subject, since the method of change establishes the character of the design.

Any pattern may be enlarged in size or reduced

FIGURE 1–56
Woven Coverlet.
Index of American Design. National Gallery of Art, Washington, D.C.

until it reads as a visual texture. It is not one size, but a combination of sizes that have a basis of related measure in common that is the material of Scale-change. The concern is two-fold: the contrast of size and the tensions that such opposition creates, and the new pattern forms that emerge from the surface. In the new surface which is created by the opposition of its contrasting pattern forms, the Baule cloth is just such a design. It goes beyond superimposing two patterns and becomes a new pattern which, indeed, is "more than the sum of its parts."

FIRST MOVE: SUBDIVIDING THE GRID

To change scale we must observe the measure of the grid unit and divide it into smaller equal units, or combine it with itself to form larger units. Between large and small scale units we may find one or two intermediate sizes that are workable. If the area is reduced, more design units are used within it; if the area is enlarged, then fewer design units are used. As the grid is reduced in scale and units are fit within the original measure of the grid layout size, an *intergrid* system is formed composed of a series of sizes that relate incrementally to one another and establish a basis for alignments when the grids are combined. It is the use of this series of related sizes that allows for sequential movement in scale on the surface. Complicated though it may sound, the method is very simple to apply. After the illustrations have been studied and understood, some sketching on graph paper should bring the whole process into focus. Not only are the simple formal combinations of sizes interesting in themselves, but when the possibility of developing work for Percentages and Manipulations within the format of Scale-change occurs, very rich, complex patterned surfaces can be developed.

As in all the games, first moves first. The first thing is to understand clearly how to make an inter-grid. If it is not done properly the necessary joining of various sizes will be thrown off and the smooth flow of contrasting sizes will be lost. In Figure 1-57 the single size unit used in all the preceding games is shown at the upper left. The diagram at the upper right includes this unit and shows an enlargement of it made by combining four standard units into a single large unit with two other subdivisions, each of which increases the number of grid units, but decreases the size of the design unit. There has to be some numerical commonality between the units no matter what their number of divisions may be because this is how the joins that make varied scale relationships possible take place. For example, the diagram shows four sizes;

FIGURE 1–57
Scale-change diagrams.

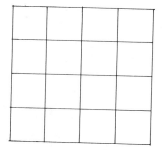
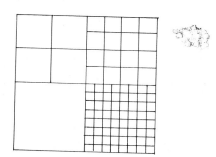

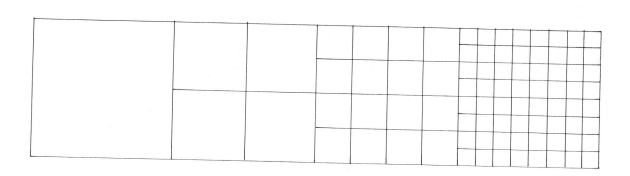

PATTERN

the upper left square contains four grid units of the same size as those shown in the grid to the left, which will be used as the standard division from which all intergrid sizes will be made. Four standard units fit into the largest area in the lower left of the diagram, showing an increase in scale. The right-hand areas show a decrease in scale: by dividing the standard unit size in quarters, 16 units are produced in the same area, and by dividing those units in quarters, 64 units are produced. A linear arrangement of the related units is shown in the lower part of the illustration: Four basic units are the common denominator for an increase or a decrease, which makes it possible to interchange areas within a repeat, or to position units in order by aligning them along the divisions common to all the design units.

To divide the areas further, and make 144 units, is hard on the eyes and the nerves, and is really unnecessary to play the game. What is necessary is to create three workable sizes—small, medium, and large—since the intermediate size performs the important function of the transition; without it only a contrast of size exists that will not give a sequential change in scale. Also, the intergrid series is a framework meant to be amplified with shape development, and if the preoccupation with intergrids becomes too involved the final patterns will be unnecessarily fussy and complicated with no more design merit than they would have if based upon a simpler approach.

TRANSITIONAL SCALE

The point in Scale-change is to develop a fluctuation and balance of visual interest through the contrast of large and small over the surface, unified by using an intermediate scale. A basic pattern rhythm is established by the repetition of large-scale design units and a counterrhythm by small-scale units—the rhythmic change is joined in the intermediate scale. As finished patterns are created, the surface takes on a dimension other than flat and appears to have areas that place forward or behind other areas, giving a fluctuation in depth due to differences in surface density produced by the varying scales. The phenomenon of visual gray appears spontaneously through the contrast of sharp dark-light in large-scale areas with a more diffuse reading in small-scale areas.

BASIC DIAGRAMS

With a set of intergrids and a shape at hand, the next move is to develop some surfaces with them. The next series of illustrations shows several methods of con-

structing repeats by combining different scales. The illustrations do not include a finished design unit, and are presented as basic moves, certainly not the whole game. The first set of examples, particularly, is meant to be used as a means of clarifying the visual events that may occur while playing Scale-change. Read all the examples shown as a sequence of development that establishes a visual vocabulary of variations using the same primary elements. Scale-change is an invitation to invent with and extend the pattern materials that have been used previously in a series of theme-and-variation designs. Working directly with the visual materials is the soundest method of generating new ideas. Once fundamental moves are understood, design possibilities occur to the designer, and a range of alternatives is produced as a spontaneous by-product of the design process. More ideas than those presented in the examples will occur as the work of individual pattern makers progresses since, as in all the games, Scale-change is not a matter of creating a single design to formula, but a series of designs based on the possibilities suggested by the relationships established in the first moves.

Figure 1-58 repeats the alignment of the scale

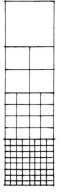
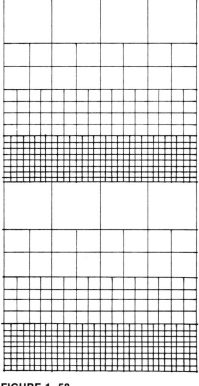

FIGURE 1–58
Scale-change diagrams.

GAME E: SCALE-CHANGE

sequence shown in Figure 1-57 as a vertical rather than a horizontal movement from small to large, including two transitional sizes. The large unit can be placed top or bottom so the scale runs from largest to smallest upward or downward. Such repositioning will not change the effect of the surface on a large area: a series of horizontal stripes. Or, the repeat can be turned to make a field of vertical stripes that move incrementally from large scale to small scale.

A more interesting idea is presented in Figure 1-59, in which the second row of the pattern shows the repeat flipped to make a compound stripe. The dominant stripe on the finished field would be that of the high scale contrast between largest and smallest, with the intermediate scales receding into the surface—an idea related to the handling of the design elements in the Baule cloth. Figure 1-59 shows the repeat given a quarter-turn to enlarge the design unit,

FIGURE 1–59
Scale-change diagrams.

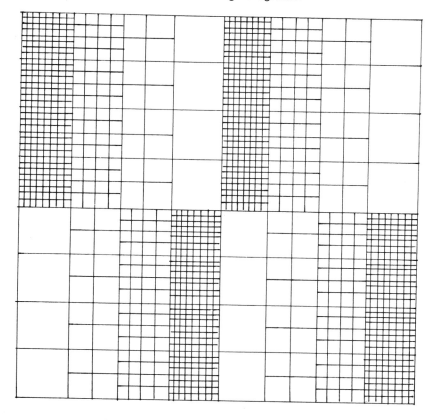

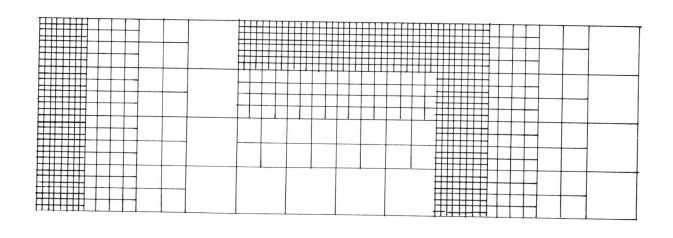

which could then be repeated evenly over the surface or alternated in the next adjoining row of units to give a different surface effect.

The size sequence does not have to be used only in the alignment shown at the upper left in Figure 1-60, but may be rearranged as shown at the upper right in the figure to vary the positions of the contrasts, and then used on the same pattern forms shown in the preceding figures, or on new ones. The lower diagram in Figure 1-60 shows one method of handling such a design unit—a rotation making a design unit of four grid units. This could be repeated evenly down and across the surface, or the second row could be alternated, or other variations used according to the methods already described for the other games. Rather than using three contrasts in four scale sizes, the sequence can be reduced to two contrasts using three sizes. For example, the upper diagram in Figure 1-61 shows nine grid units combined to make a single unit using large, medium, and small scales in equal amounts and composed symmetrically. The lower diagram shows a pattern structure created by rotation and alternation, which yields a distribution of sizes over the surface.

Figure 1-62 omits the largest size and uses the remaining sizes in a design unit composed on a diagonal axis with equal amounts of each of the three scales. One possible arrangement is shown in the center of Figure 1-62, a naive but appealing pattern form, hackneyed from overuse. Another pattern developed from the same design unit is shown in the lower part of the illustration. Other design units may be composed asymmetrically with unequal amounts of large, medium, and small used, but unless the balance between the amounts is carefully controlled and not allowed to become too extreme in contrast, the smallest areas will tend to spot out on the surface.

In using a scale sequence—a series of sizes in combination—points of emphasis in the surfaces created from them will always occur at the lines of greatest contrast. When small-scale units fall next to large-scale units the difference in size will draw more attention and have more effect on the pattern structure than the lines of contrast between more closely related scale areas. It is an amplification of the dark-light contrast seen and used in all the preceding work, and is as important in Scale-change as in any other game.

FIGURE 1–60
Scale-change repeat development.

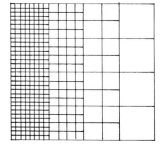 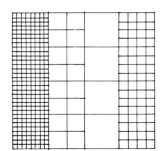 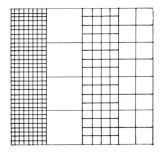

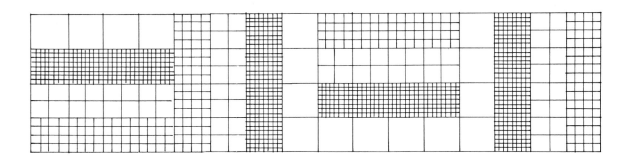

GAME E: SCALE-CHANGE

The interplay of scale should be experienced in warm-up exercises, such as those shown here, without developing shape content or completed pattern surfaces until some groundwork in possible arrangements has been done.

Some experimental sketching on graph paper with a pen or pencil will show that the grid unit must be used in multiples to make a single design unit that may contain three or four contrasting scales. Rather than being thought of as sixteen separate units of different size—as shown in Figure 1-59, for example—the entire combination should be used as a single unit. Manipulating the unit will produce patterns based on stripes and checkerboards, plaid-like designs, half-drops, diagonals, gradations, and effects of texture on the surface. But once composed, symmetrically or asymmetrically, the unit must be repeated evenly to make a patterned surface that is equally balanced.

FIGURE 1–61
Scale-change, symmetrically composed repeat.

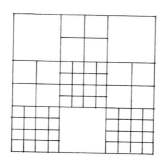

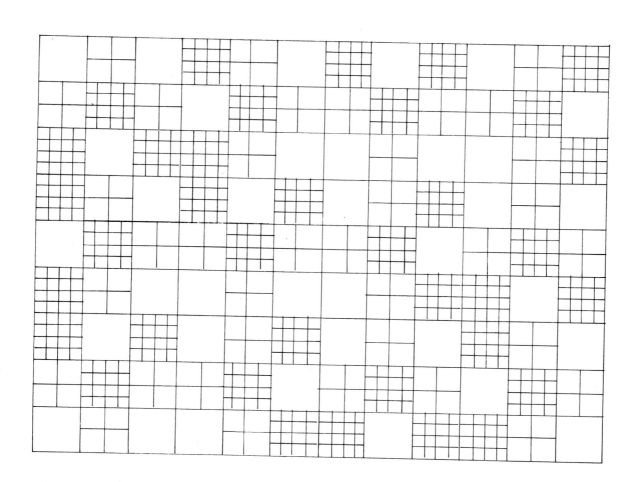

FIGURE 1–62
Scale-change, symmetrically composed repeat.

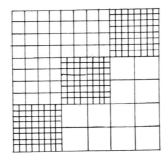

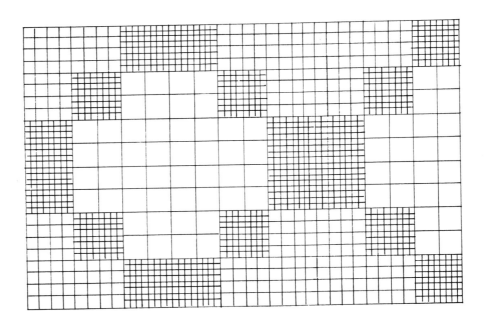

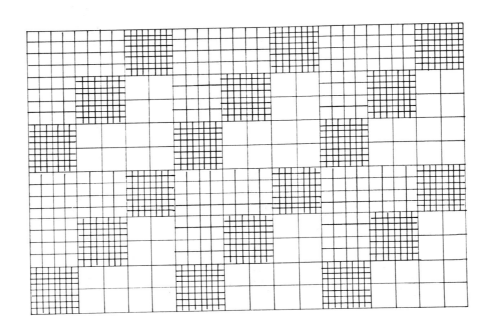

GAME E: SCALE-CHANGE

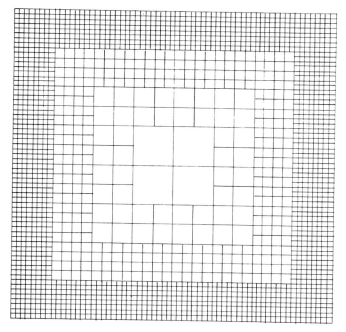

FIGURE 1–63
Scale-change,
symmetrically composed repeat.

A SCALE-CHANGE SEQUENCE

In the following illustrations a single shape—a variation on a triangle—has been manipulated to create a series of repeats composed in scale sequence. The first example, Figure 1-64, shows groupings of the unit arranged as a checkerboard, and without variation in scale. It is one of a series of trial pieces made to examine some possible combinations. The shape has been combined with itself to form a thick curved shape having a definite diagonal direction, which gives an effect of interwoven zigzag areas on the finished surface.

The shape is stated by itself, as the largest unit, in Figure 1-65, and then used in two smaller scales for the other parts of the repeat. The entire repeat is composed of four small-scale units, seven intermediate units, and five large units, placed asymmetrically, and designed to be repeated across and down a given area to make a patterned surface. The composition of the repeat is skillfully handled, with emphases distributed throughout the balanced layout. The large dark-light units are emphatic but do not overwhelm the others,

FIGURE 1–64
Sequence. Student project by Madeline Eng, designer.

FIGURE 1–65

FIGURE 1–66

Three student projects on Sequence
by Madeline Eng, designer.

and the diagonal, wave-like motion in the design unit is countered nicely by the right-angled grid structure. Surface depth is minimal, but the density of the small-scale units contrasted to the large shapes enriches the surface reading. The transitional scale is dominant in an amount which supports the contrast of large and small. It is a simple, well-realized surface.

The design elements do not coalesce in the repeat shown in Figure 1-66. Although the shape combinations are interesting in the manner in which they reach across the grid lines to complete themselves, there are too many different kinds. The grid is neither fully absorbed into the combinations, nor used in the frank manner shown in Figure 1-65. Angles, curves, straight lines, curved lines and zigzag lines compete, and there is not a controlling dominant movement in the layout. The middle scale is not utilized in an effective way, and the small-scale units have the appearance of arbitrary groups on the surface. The surface would have had a more integrated effect if the large shapes had been edited to one or two that moved consistently over it, and the middle scale been composed in units that related to the simple structure of the small-scale areas to join them with the curvilinear character of the large units.

Figure 1-67 shows a well-realized repeat that is successful for the very reasons that the previous example was not: the shape combination is simple and used consistently; there is a clear dominant movement

FIGURE 1–67

over the surface that is not confused with the grid, but absorbs it; and the joinings between sizes appear natural and effortless. There would be a discrepancy between the subdirections of the units when read from left to right if the area was supposed to be complete in itself. However, when it is seen as a repeat, the subordinate horizontal movement in small-scale units would act as a controlled countermovement to the dominant curving diagonal of the middle and large-scale areas on a large surface.

Figure 1-67 is a good visual definition of a *composed repeat*, in which the combination of elements is complex enough in itself to indicate that it should be used in the elementary one-to-one alignment on the surface to make a large pattern. Rotating it would negate the effectiveness of its movements, as would reversing it. It is meant to be used as seen, but it is not finished. It can only be completed by being repeated, when its movements and submovements will clarify, and the variety in surface depth, created by high and low dark-light contrast areas, will be realized.

The Scale-change game draws upon the same pattern ideas used throughout all of the games and reforms them in relation to the sequence of size established by the intergrids. The manipulation is in the grid, and pattern repeats are composed from the interplay of large and small and transitional sizes. Shapes, design units, organizations from earlier patterns should be tried within the format of Scale-change. They, in turn, will become the source of further ideas. For example, taking the shape used in Game C (Manipulations)—the ubiquitous triangle—and a way of handling it from Figure 1-46 in Game D (Visual Gray), and combining them with an intergrid system, it is possible to compose a repeat such as that suggested in Figure 1-68: a right-angled triangle made up of many small triangles. In this repeat three sizes are used, all of which are composed by combining the smallest figure with itself. The repeat could as easily be realized in strong dark-light and visual gray, or reorganized into different combinations of triangles, as alternatives to what is shown in the example. The repeat could be cut biaxially and recomposed in various ways, used as four design units, or it could be simply stated as in the alignment suggested by the repeat shown in Figure 1-67. The point is that there are many possibilities for the individual designer to discover—shapes, contrasts, combinations, transitions, sizes—that can be orchestrated into new pattern forms through Scale-change.

A PATTERN STRUCTURE ANALYSIS: SYNTHESIZING THE ELEMENTS

One of the oldest Japanese crafts is the stencil, paste resist, and dip dyeing method used to decorate lengths of fabric. The stencils, called *kata-gami*, are made from mulberry bark paper precisely cut or punched with the desired patterns. Often a web of silk filaments is layered between two identically cut stencils to hold finely detailed areas in place and give support to large open areas in the design. The stencil edges must be cut with great exactness since the stencil is usually meant to be used as a single repeat in a continuous design joining accurately at each end, or sometimes at the sides when meant to cover widths of cloth. The most common method of using the stencil is to place it in registration on a carefully prepared smooth length of fabric and force rice-paste resist through its openings with a spatula-like tool. Once the resist dries the entire cloth is dipped in dye, and at a later stage in the finishing the fabric resist is removed by washing, leaving areas the color of the cloth adjacent to dyed areas where no resist was used.

Kata-gami have come to be regarded as works of art in themselves. Many have been collected and are exhibited as fine examples of one form of traditional Japanese craftsmanship. Although the design and execution of these stencils is but one step in a complicated process of textile printing, to the modern eye they appear as complete designs and are appreciated

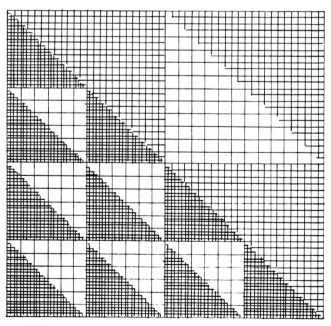

FIGURE 1–68
Visual gray, Scale-change superimposition.

FIGURE 1–69
Kata-gami: Arrow Feathers. 46.7 × 34 cm.
Courtesy of Cooper-Hewitt Museum, The Smithsonian Institution's
National Museum of Design.

as such. However, it must be kept in mind that they are pattern repeats, or units, meant to combine with themselves end to end, side to side, or both, and as such they are carefully planned to align at the edge to create a continuous surface when used.

The fine example shown in Figure 1-69 shows a highly stylized "Arrow Feather" motif often found in such stencils. It is a bold shape, geometric and symmetrical in design. The organization of the overall design, as in the Baule cloth, is that of a stripe, equal in width except for the central small-scale stripe which contains a half-unit at its left margin making seven small stripes repeating the seven of each half of the larger and lighter value "feather."

The design's organization consists of a series of small stripes grouped and used as a visual support for smaller and larger stylized feather units to create a reading of many changes of scales in the width of the stripe. The basic rhythm of the piece is the composition of seven small stripes in the center which are roughly equal in width to each half of the parallelograms that form the feather shape. The complete large feather is composed of fourteen stripes. All the stripes are equal in width except those at the edge, which are half-width and make a border. The repeat is meant to be made on the upper and lower edges of the short dimension. It is difficult to conceive of the piece joining at all four edges; more likely the stencil was used for printing a long strip of material since, when joined at the long sides, the small scale arrow stripe does not repeat in rhythmic alternation. Therefore, the stripes at the long sides can be looked upon as borders meant to frame and finish the center. This clarifies the basic numerical rhythm of seven throughout the central section and its break at the edges.

There are sixteen small-scale and two large-scale feather units running the length of the stencil, making a dramatic change in size ratio of 1 to 8. Such a contrast in size without the rhythmic support of the even pattern base of fine linear elements that are used consistently across the surface might easily cancel itself, fail in its visual effect, and become only an unresolved contrast.

Large- and small-scale units are built upon the same incremental foundation, a parallelogram, which when reversed and combined with itself makes an elongated chevron shape—the "feather" unit. Visual gray is particularly well realized in the design. By reducing the large feather unit from light to a light-middle value, the tension of high contrast is maintained without being overwhelming. These areas contrast with the small scale high contrast feather units making them appear most intense in value contrast.

Further, the large feather units integrate with one another in sharing a transition at their common edge—a line of middle value which firmly anchors the large units to the surface. By handling the large-scale units in this restrained sequence of value and concentrating the hard dark-light contrasts in the smaller units, the surface appears to have levels. The smaller stripe appears on top, or forward from the larger stripe, and when viewed from a distance, the feather shapes are reduced in visual importance and become subordinate to the dominant pattern idea: Stripe. What attracts the observer's eye first, the important dark arrow feather unit, becomes part of the stripe and equates and exchanges with the other elements of the design as an essential part, but not the whole, of the pattern.

Composing dynamic movements within a field so they are contained is a matter of maintaining sensitive control of dominant directions and counterdirections. It is interesting to observe how the designer of the stencil achieved this control. The area is active, it moves in a vigorous way up and is countered by an equally assertive movement down. This equal movement is established by repetition of the elongated chevron—the arrow-like shapes are directional pointers. The up and down movement is placed with the more agitated small-scale movements in the central stripe and the borders, which appear on a different surface plane—forward of the plane of the large motif. Both stripes possess a harmony of sameness in shape content and placement, but contrast dramatically in scale, or relative size. The foundation for the visual activity in movement is found in the rhythm of repetition in the stripes, the seven to seven measure, the manipulation of the same design shape, and equal balance in dark-light in the small-scale units, and equal balance in dark-middle values in the large scale units. They are the constants of the pattern. Further, the subordinate lateral movement, from small to large in alternation across the dominant direction of the surface creates a counterrhythm, not only slowing the vertical movement, but enriching its effect through contrast while controlling it.

Many of the balance characteristics of a well-realized patterned surface can be seen in this small example of *kata-gami*. It shows the understanding and use of an even metrical base. The movements of the surface are contained and controlled. There is an exchange of dominant and subordinate design elements, and a balance of proportionate dark-light areas. It is an excellent example of the symmetrical mode of pattern in its best applications: equal movement of equal elements over the surface.

DISTRIBUTION

EQUAL MOVEMENT OF UNEQUAL ELEMENTS OVER THE SURFACE

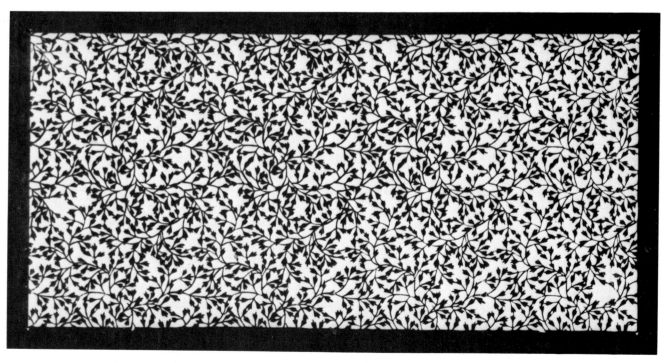

FIGURE 2–1
Kata-gami: Leafy Vine. 18 × 35.4 cm.
Courtesy of Cooper-Hewitt Museum, The Smithsonian Institution's
National Museum of Design.

Distribution deals with the rhythmic reorganization of pattern structure. It involves movements of unequal elements which are equalized over the surface through the interplay of countermovements between them rather than by an even repetition of identical design units. Different movements combine and exchange between the distributed elements, balancing each other, so that the finished surfaces appear as uniform as those of pattern. The movements of Pattern and Distribution express rhythmic orders—the basis of all surface organization.

The *kata-gami* shown in Figure 2-1 is designed as an interlacement of lines and dots spaced around various sizes of irregular light shapes. It is difficult to focus long on any particular area on the surface since it appears as a visual wander without a stop. There is an occasional pause at one of the eccentric light shapes formed where curved lines and small dot-like leaf shapes join, but the interdependence and equal emphasis given to these three elements, and their distribution within the design, creates a continuous

movement without interruptions over the surface. The light shapes vary in size from large to small, in evenly arranged contrasts, without emphasis on one size or the other. The curvilinear elements move vigorously through the design, each countering the other, enclosing movements within the surface. Throughout, the dots and masses extend the action of the lines and define the light areas. However, upon careful looking, it can be seen that the design is made up of smaller areas, identically composed, within a grid structure; particular shapes repeat at regular, measured intervals. It is the skillful use of similar, but not identical, elements within each grid unit that disguises the small repeat, and the large area of the complete stencil repeat appears as a single self-contained plane.

CONTRAST TO PATTERN

This organization of evenly distributed but contrasting elements, differs sharply from that of a standard checkerboard arrangement, with its minimal visual vocabulary of a single dark-light exchange in even alternation over a surface. It differs, too, from any of the surfaces developed in Pattern—Figures 1-24, 1-34, or 1-67, for example—where a simple rhythm of repetition of even the most complex of composed repeats is the basis of organization. The *kata-gami* shows an arrangement of elements in an equilibrium maintained by movements balanced by countermovements. The freely developed surface shown in Figure 2-2 is made up of brush strokes all similar in character,

FIGURE 2–2
Distributed surface—
ink study.

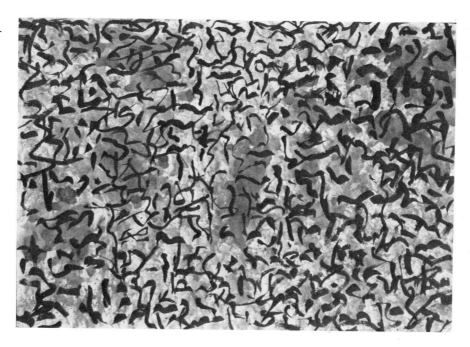

DISTRIBUTION

but with each slightly different from the others. It is not based on a grid foundation, as is the *kata-gami*, but the idea of a uniform surface composed of evenly distributed design elements without an obvious statement of measured repeat is common to both.

Although the grid is used as a foundation for surfaces developed in Distribution, its final effect on the surfaces is quickly minimized by the arrangement of elements. The American crazy quilt, Figure 2-3, is made up of many small patches that certainly give the appearance of even distribution. Even the symmetrical motif at the upper center of the quilt becomes subordinate to the overall activity of the surface. Nevertheless, the design clearly states its grid base, 15 units in all, rather than absorbing it. In itself, this is not a bad thing—in fact, it was probably what the designer wanted—however, for the intention of Distribution, the second quilt, Figure 2-4, is better de-

FIGURE 2–3
Crazy Quilt.
Courtesy of The Seattle Art Museum, Gift of Mrs. Harriet L. French.

veloped as an all-over surface, although no grid at all is used as a foundation. The examples represent extremes that are interesting in themselves: the first creates an interesting visual tension between the apparently erratic patches organized within a regular grid, and the second shows a balanced visual scramble over the surface. They can be related to the preceding examples of *kata-gami* and free study. All of the examples are worth examination, but the structure of Distribution lies between the extremes shown, rather than at one end or the other.

PATTERN-LIKE

Distribution is based upon Pattern, and can be best understood by seeing how it relates and contrasts to Pattern. The basic structure of all patterned surfaces is that of an even repetitive rhythm. The concept of Distribution is that of continual but contained movement—not randomness, but a *pattern-like* functioning of the parts of the design. A clearer visual distinction can be made by comparing any of the dark-light surfaces from Manipulations with the *kata-gami* shown

FIGURE 2–4
Patchwork Quilt.
Index of American Design. National Gallery of Art, Washington, D.C.

DISTRIBUTION

in Figure 2-1. Distribution is closely related to Pattern since the design elements share an identity that gives them an appearance of sameness, but they do not repeat exactly. The solid, measured, one-to-one repeat, characteristic of simple pattern is missing. Its function is replaced by that of interacting movements between the design elements: the tempo is one of evenness over the surface created by movements that are countered by equal and opposite movements, without exact repetition.

Three *molas* from the San Blas Indians of Panama are shown in Figures 2-5, 2-6, and 2-7. They should be compared with each other to see how the idea of Distribution is evolved from a Pattern foundation. A similar basic motif is used in each *mola*, with variations in each of the three examples, to develop its surface. The first, Figure 2-5, is very close to a plain pattern statement: a complex design unit evenly spaced on the surface, in an equal exchange of dark and light. The second, Figure 2-6, combines areas that are not equal, but share the same line width, and repeat the same turning movement in line. The top section of the design seems to grow out of the more regulated arrangement of the bottom section, but

FIGURE 2–5
Mola.

takes on a different kind of relationship to the total piece through the placement and interaction of the linear motif; a very approximate symmetrical arrangement unifies the two parts of the surface. It becomes a composition of areas distributed over the surface. One's attention is on the all-over actions of the field as they balance each other, which is a contrast to the visual control of repetition seen in the first example.

The repetition of consistent shapes creates a strong "patterned" impression in the third *mola* shown, Figure 2-7, but an even and controlled repeat—a consistent metrical rhythm—is absent. The result suggests pattern, but it is not pattern. Rather, it is a balanced arrangement of closely related but continually varied elements, which is characteristic of Distribution. It is in this sense that it is "pattern-like." The maze design of the *mola* is made up of like elements varied in size, put into an interesting and rugged irregular order, based upon the interaction of strong vertical and horizontal intersections, from which the stepped rhythm is developed as a control. The idea of a regular repeat is secondary. A comparison with Figure 2-6 should clarify the contrast between areas made up of similiar elements that are distributed evenly

FIGURE 2–6
Mola.

FIGURE 2–7
Mola.

within it, and areas in which the elements, though identical in character—if not in exact size and shape—are combined in a more structured arrangement, which becomes compositional. The elements in Figure 2-6 are unequal in visual weight and placement, and mass to form superior dominant shapes, establishing centers of visual emphasis rather than creating a uniform, uninterrupted surface, such as that shown in Figure 2-7, which is the quality of Distribution. Further clarification of the differences can be seen by comparing Figure 1-24 with the *kata-gami*. Figure 2-1, and the *mola*, Figure 2-6. In each there is an identity of shape content, and each fully develops its surface, but uses a different method to do so.

The surface shown in Figure 2-8 is another good example of free distribution of elements—here a dot—besides the brush and ink study and the crazy quilt examples (Figures 2-2 and 2-3). As a whole, the surface has variety and interest in the movements made up by the alignment of the dots, and the stress and release caused by their varying densities. There are no obvious stops, no strong single directional movements, no superior shapes emerging from the massed elements, and it certainly does not appear as a regular pattern organization. It should be pointed out that although the dots on this surface are dissimilar in size and are in balanced distribution over the surface, an edge has been developed around the field which gives

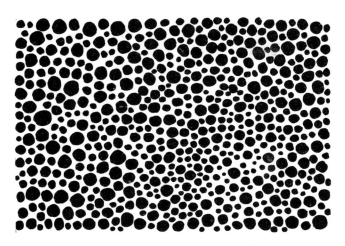

FIGURE 2–8
Dot—ink study.

the appearance of a frame. If the area is meant to be selfcontained—complete as it is—there can be no objection to this margination. However, if the area is meant to be used as a single repeat on a larger, all-over surface, the idea of a continuous and even distribution would be lost, and the rectangular framework of the combined units would control and dominate the resulting surface—an effect similar to that of the crazy quilt made up of fifteen square units.

FIGURE AND FIELD

Although the grid is the foundation of both, the placement of design units within the grid is one of continual variation in Distribution rather than that of consistent placement, as in Pattern. This difference gives a directionless character to distributed surfaces, such as those seen in Figure 2-1 and 2-18, which contrasts to the strong directional movements frequently produced in Pattern games when design unit joins design unit, as shown in Figure 1-31, particularly. This makes the initial moves in Distribution games more complex than those of Pattern since the entire field is always in the process of becoming completed. No single area is defined until its adjacent areas are defined, and the games are played as continuities, with no part complete without the definition of another part. Just as in poetry one line is often dependent upon the following lines for completion of sense, rhythm, and form, in design a patterned surface is not complete until all the design units are in position and become mutually defining, and the surface can be understood

as a whole. But the complexities of simple symmetrical rhythms are not those of asymmetrical rhythms, where the awareness of the total page and the interactions of all its compositional elements must be in balance at once. There is no part of a composed surface that is less or more important than any other part: one thing has the same value as another. In a traditional figure-field relationship, that part or portion that is to support and express the figure—the field—will be effective only if it supports and completes the composition. Less or more will entirely alter the result. As such, the field cannot be a passive support for the dynamic of the figure, but must have an active function in the entire design of the surface. Here, the traditional description of figure and field has been replaced by the simple observation that everything counts: everything is connected to everything else, and the connecting relationships are the design.

Unless this general idea, this unifying viewpoint exists, there is little to be gained by criticizing particular parts of a design. If all the parts are of equal importance as they interact with one another, then the entire area must be seen at once as it has been put down as a self-contained organization. Are the parts working together to create a single unified impression? Any attempt to rectify particular areas is valuable only insofar as it relates to the whole and calls attention to the entire concept and how it has been felt and stated. Then the area that seems out of relationship can be taken into the general context of the design and corrected from that standpoint. When criticism focusses on details, with attention to parts rather than to the whole, the result is likely to be no more than a piecing together or a patching up.

The relationship of connecting design elements as they move together to form a complete surface is the particular emphasis in Distribution. The thinking is the same as that required when drawing from the human body: one shape anticipates and defines another shape in a rhythmic continuum, and this relationship between the shapes must be understood before one is able to draw. In the conventional study of the torso shown in Figure 2-9, the twisted axis of the pose gives a dynamic quality to the figure; however, it remains an active figure on a passive field. The areas surrounding the drawing serve to define the figure, but full attention has been given to the figure rather than to a completed surface. This is not true of the seated figure shown in Figure 2-10. A comparison of this drawing with Figure 2-9 shows immediately that here the entire page is being composed. Although figure and field exchange is not equal, all the areas of the surface are considered as being interdependent in the composition.

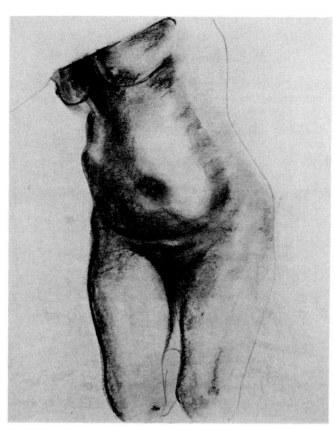

FIGURE 2–9
Figure drawing.

FIGURE 2–10
Figure drawing.

The third study, Figure 2-11, shows a simplification and exaggeration of the salient parts of the form; details irrelevant to the intention of the composition have been eliminated. The shapes suggest a human form through their contour and position. The ground and the shapes are interlocked; they define each other more clearly here than in either of the other drawings. All the shapes have a distinct character of their own, and the dark-light exchange is a significant element in the composition. The balance of dark and light is very close to the approach taken when creating the design unit for pattern surfaces. Each part of the plane depends upon an adjacent part for definition, and the representation of the model is subordinate to the overall composition of the page. After playing the first game in Distribution look at this sequence again. Using abstract shapes that relate to geometry may seem different from handling recognizable forms from nature, but a comparison with the experience of main-

taining a balance of unequal elements over a surface will show that the fundamentals are the same whether one is dealing with pure pattern shapes or known subject matter: concentration on the relationships between the elements that are being composed. On that basis, the approach to drawing a figure is the same as that taken in the free study in ink on paper shown in Figure 2-12. A strong wave-like horizontal movement dominates and pushes past the right- and left-hand edges of the field. However, the distribution of the design elements is balanced, and the entire surface is developed completely in dark and light. The dark could be put down on a light ground, or the light on a dark ground—one can focus on dark or light masses at will. Using the entire surface, activating all of its parts—making them count as integral parts of the whole—is basic in Pattern, Distribution, and Composition.

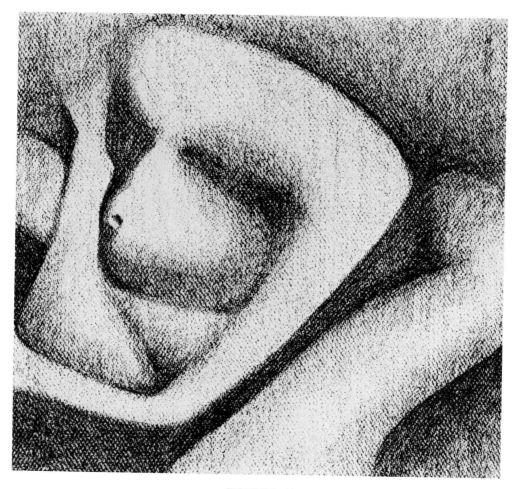

FIGURE 2–11
Figure drawing by Chris Baumgartner.

FIGURE 2–12
Line—ink study.

SYMMETRY, BALANCE, AND RHYTHM

Proportionate balance between the component parts of the design is referred to as their symmetry. It is a broad term, generally used to describe the stability of the parts when they are combined, as well as the method by which they are equated with each other to form a whole, or a unity of visual impression. Symmetry is often used to specifically contrast a centered visual organization with one that is asymmetrical. Used in that sense it refers to an organizing axis that divides the plane or form into even proportions, commonly two equal halves, one half being the mirror image of the other. Whether vertically or horizontally divided, such an arrangement is called bilateral, or, if the plane is divided into four equal parts around a cross axis, biaxial, as shown in Figure 2-13. Whatever the refinements of organization may be, bisymmetry requires that there must be a clearly controlling axis established, around which the composing elements interact. Asymmetry usually refers to a series of visual

FIGURE 2–13
Bead work and embroidery panel, Afghanistan.

DISTRIBUTION

forces or impressions, the combination of which reads as an organized whole which does not depend upon a clearly stated focus in its structure. Rather, it is a distribution of visual weights around a center, or related centers, that are read as being in a constant flux of visual interchange, or movements that maintain their balance—symmetry in the broad sense—through continuous exchange: movement to countermovement. There are many elaborations of the definitions of these terms but, in the main, they refer to these two prevailing modes of balance in art forms: the way things are put together and, consequently, how they are looked at. Whether the surface is developed symmetrically or asymmetrically, it must be consistent within its mode to make a coherent whole. Most criticism of surface designs that do not seem satisfactory is directed towards methods of obtaining this consistency, or balance, within the relationships of the operating visual elements.

All patterns are symmetrical, that is, they are regular in their structure, and maintain their equilibrium through the even arrangement of their composing elements. Established pattern forms such as the checkerboard, the stripe, and the S-shaped curve—shown in Figure 2-14—presuppose a symmetrical mode of balance. All the patterned surfaces created when playing Percentages or Manipulations are symmetrical in the sense that they are uniformly balanced arrangements of like elements. The difference between a surface pattern produced by playing Percentages or Manipulations or Scale-change and those developed by playing Distribution games is that the distributed surfaces are not the result of the symmetry of stance, but of the symmetry of movement. Simple repetition is the functioning method of the first, transition of the second. Rhythmic variation is what determines the kind of symmetrical balance in each.

Patterns produced when playing the games in Distribution remain symmetrical in their finished results, for though the elements of the pattern may be unequal in size, area, or visual weight, their final placement is the solution to the problem of establish-

FIGURE 2–14
Kata-gami: Autumn Grasses, Bush Clover,
and Butterflies. 36.4 × 34.8 cm.
Courtesy of Cooper-Hewitt Museum, The Smithsonian Institution's
National Museum of Design.

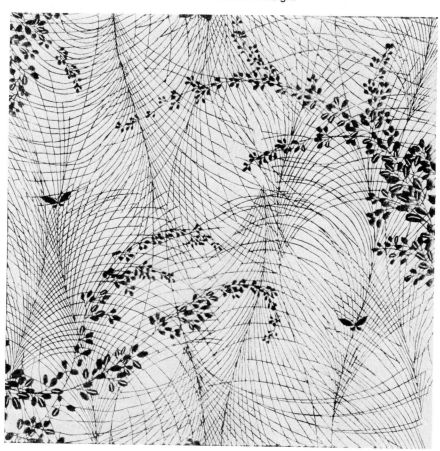

ing an even balance—or distribution—within a surface of inequalities. This is a more difficult process than playing Pattern games, and consequently the method of manipulating the surface differs considerably from that of the pattern constructions in Chapter 1. Rather than a symmetrical manipulation of like elements, it is a symmetrical manipulation of unlike elements, with emphasis not on simple repetition, but upon the tensions and transitions between unequal elements held in balance through their equal distribution over the surface. Although it is quite possible to repeat the finished design—which may be handled as a large and complex single design unit, as shown later in this section—the method of developing a surface remains distinct from that used in Pattern games; however, in both Pattern and Distribution, the relationship between the design elements is essentially a rhythmic one.

Rhythm, the incremental movement characterized by regularity and recurrence, can be as obvious as the three-quarter time of a waltz, as structured as the stress and release of iambic pentameter in verse, as visually insistent as the dark-light exchange of a checkerboard, or as subtle as the passage of time. Whether simple or complex, rhythm is the basis for organizing and balancing the relationships between similiar or diverse elements, and establishing the fundamental condition of unity between them which renders the completed form. In Pattern, placement is equal and develops as an even regular beat that is continuous over the surface. Distribution depends upon the equilibrium between dissimiliar elements to develop a balanced series of discontinuous movements to form a surface. It is not as regular in tempo as Pattern since it is not composed of equal units, but of combinations of movements, each anticipating the next which defines and completes it in sequence. Rather than the measured symmetrical balance of dark-light elements which define Pattern, Distribution is the asymmetrically balanced dispersion of elements over the surface.

Elements articulating a surface are always seen in combinations. There is never just one thing, one element, existing in isolation. And no element in itself is more important than its connection to any other. A dot placed on a plane serves to define the areas of that plane, as the plane defines the location and size of the dot. Their combination creates a visual context within which the relationship of the two is judged. If the dot is shifted in location on the plane, the surrounding areas redistribute in relation to it. For example, placing a dot to the side activates the planar area asymmetrically. In both, the relationships are defined by contrasting size and position of the surface

FIGURE 2–15
Dots.

elements. It is a continuation of pattern shape development, where a dark shape placed on a light field defines the light field as a complementary shape, and the dark-light combination creates the design unit, which, when repeated, forms the pattern surface. In both, the relationship is one of contrast: dark against light, light against dark, small to large, dot to plane, round to square. These connections of contrasts and the manner in which they are made is always of greater significance than the particular elements that are being connected, because they are the raw material of the structure of the surface.

DESIGNING A UNIT

The scale of the design units used for Distribution differs markedly from those of Pattern which uses planar shapes occupying 30 to 50 percent of the grid unit to complete the dark-light exchange. Pattern game units make edge contact with at least two sides of the grid unit to make joins and combinations possible. Although these arrangements may take on strong directional movements over the surface of the pattern field, the design units themselves are usually contained planes. In contrast, the design unit used to play Distribution is an unequal combination of line and plane in which the percentage of dark and light is in high contrast; Figure 2-16 shows a comparison between them. This contrast makes it possible to arrive at a variety of placements that could not be achieved by using only planar elements. It is interesting to notice that the combination of contained planar elements in Pattern often produces strong linear movements on the surface, while the directional characteristics of the design elements in Distribution are combined to produce an active but directionless surface. Dark-light balance in Distribution is not concerned with equalizing dark with light on the surface; either dark or light will dominate in amount depending

FIGURE 2–16
Comparison of planar pattern
and linear distribution elements.

upon whether the work is done on a field of one value weight or the other. However, the interaction of the two is as important in Distribution as it is in Pattern. Unless full attention is given to the shapes that are being produced by the interaction of dark and light placement, the surface will fail. Light shapes will be formed by the placement of darks and will take directions that must integrate with the rhythmic movement to countermovement characteristic of the surfaces in Distribution. Work can never be done with dark or light alone, but with the combination of the two, just as it was done in Pattern games.

It appears instinctive with anyone first learning to draw to manually describe the object being drawn in terms of its apparent outline. The greatest amount of visual information seems to reside at the boundary of form and space. Such a beginning does not always lead to a convincing perception of form, nor does it lead to that analytic-understanding seeing that produces good drawing. Nevertheless, line is one of the most powerful and effective of all design tools. It is

rare for a person to describe "round" with both hands cupped, as if containing the roundness of solid or volume. Most likely the gesture used will be that of an index finger describing a circle in space—a linear gesture that is simple, economic, and direct. If it is not a complete description, it gets the intended message across to the observer in a kind of visual shorthand. The action of the gesture, or of drawing a line on paper is usually an action of from-here-to there, which subsequently sets up definitions of inside-to-outside, or contained-to-excluded, or horizontal-to-vertical.

The strongest two-dimensional line work occurs when the interdependence of line and plane is understood and conveyed rather than thinking of line as a separate element—a boundary marker of a contour, or the track of a gesture alone. For example, the planar shape defined by line must, in turn, be seen as defining the line, just as one shape defined another shape in pattern work. The reciprocal actions of push-pull of planes and the directional movements of lines exist in intimate balance, regardless of whether one element or the other is emphasized in their organization.

Line is a term used to describe many varying conditions: directions, or lines of movement; an outline of a figure or a shape; a dividing line or a boundary; a border or an edge. It has been used in just such varying contexts in this book. When used in Distribution it means a mark of relatively light weight, which contrasts to the broad area of a plane. Also, just as an edge of a plane may function visually as a line, so line may function as the boundary of a plane, as well as an element in itself. Qualities of line vary as widely as those of shapes, and they make as interesting a separate study as do shapes (Figure 2-17). Some basic characteristics of line are shown in the visual examples

FIGURE 2–17
Line variations.

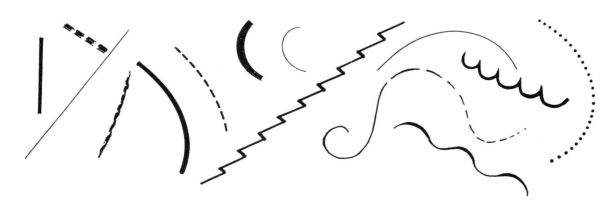

DISTRIBUTION

in this section, but they cannot be exhaustive because the possibilities are as varied as the minds behind the hands that draw them.

Strong linear directional movements over the surface were a frequent result of playing Pattern games. Created out of the potential for them in the design unit, and developed when the units were placed in combination, they appeared as by-products of Manipulation. In Distribution short, emphatic linear movements are deliberately established within the grid unit—in contrast to its right-angled construction—which become directional markings over the surface. Shapes are created from the areas between the lines: when one line is put down the entire field becomes a support for it, but shapes are articulated when other lines are put down in relation to it. This interplay of line and plane is basic, and reverses the emphasis on planar shapes in Pattern games; line is considered to be the primary design element from which planes are formed. Consequently, the dark-light balance does not equate. There is a definite dominance of either dark or light.

MOVEMENT AND COUNTERMOVEMENT

A distributed surface is developed as a whole on which elements of equal interest are placed without reference to a strict metrical repeat, or a center of control,

but in relation to the static framework of the underlying grid. The entire field reaches the observer as a complete active force without pause: movement to countermovement, in a union that reads as a single unit. Figures 2-18 and 2-19 should be compared before beginning Game A. They show the conditions that must be considered if a satisfying surface is to be produced. The dot study, Figure 2-18, is controlled by a regular but asymmetrical scattering of the various points. One's eye reads the page by moving rapidly from dot to dot over the surface. Compare it with Figure 2-19, which shows a regular symmetrical placement of equal sizes at the intersections of the grid lines. One reads it as a visual definition of the underlying grid structure. The grid has been used as a support in both examples, but each interprets it in a different way.

GAME A
THE BASIC GAME

Simple as it looks, so many factors are operating at once that Distribution may prove to be difficult to play at first. The beginning game focusses most of these factors in a basic surface manipulation: Distribution

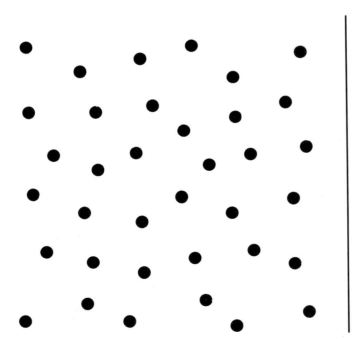

FIGURE 2–18
Asymmetric dot study.

FIGURE 2–19
Symmetric dot study.

itself. There are variations, elaborations, extensions, and inventions, but the fundamental thinking remains constant through them all. The game may be played with black and white cut paper, but an easier and more efficient method is to use a blunt-tipped felt marking pen, graph paper, and a pad of tracing paper. Rather than doing an entire area over and over again, put sheets of tracing paper over a grid drawn on graph paper and make corrections on the overlay sheets as the work progresses. Before beginning, a good preparatory exercise is to do several free studies with ink and brush on paper, such as those shown in Figures 2-2 and 2-8, to develop familiarity with the idea of even distribution.

Beforehand sketching was discouraged as a preliminary step in playing Pattern games, but for Distribution it is encouraged. To gain the direct experience of dark-light exchange it is necessary to move shapes over a grid in Pattern, and the same approach may be taken in Distribution. Preferably, however, some drawing on graph paper—to get the feel of the game—should be done before cut and paste, or drawing to finished size, is done. Do not sketch small; full size trial sketches are the most effective ones to work with. Postage stamp size sketches are of no consequence—they cannot show enough. Sketches must be large and they must be thorough. At least one-half to three-quarters of the planned finished size—if not full-size drawings—should be used, otherwise the relationship of the elements will not be clear, and no real visual information will be gained. Many preliminary sketches should be made and compared before a final design is done.

FIRST MOVES

For the first game use a grid of $1\frac{1}{2} \times 1\frac{1}{2}$ inch units, eight across and eight down, duplicating the standard format for Pattern games. Refer to Figure 2-20 to see how the design units should be composed. A heavy line, or bar, cuts across the grid unit at an angle reaching from top to bottom, or from side to side, but not from top to side, or side to bottom. In effect, the grid unit is divided into three parts: two planes formed by the position of the single line. For ease in work, a dark line on a light ground is recommended, but the procedure may be reversed if desired. When one grid unit combines with another the planar shapes will be extended from grid unit to grid unit to form new shapes. This idea of creating shapes by combining elements is exactly that of Pattern, however the significant change is in relative sizes, and the results will appear quite different from those produced in Pattern. Also,

the factor of always differentiating the position of the line is the opposite of exact repetition of position. An interesting note is that, although the line is in subordinate amount to the planar shapes, it is its position that creates the surface structure, but the multi-directional character of the surface is a combination of both elements.

Distribute the line over the entire grid, changing its position within each grid unit. Do not repeat positions; continually vary them. The point is to obtain an even distribution of elements over the surface, one without stops or holes that may be caused by repeated or paired positions, or linear movements caused by alignments.

Remember two important things when working: First, never attempt to fill the page by moving regularly over it, such as starting at the left edge and going to the right edge, or starting in a corner and progressively filling the grid downward and across. Distribute an element here, another there, working asymmetrically over the symmetrical grid. Second, stand back and look at the surface, or use a reducing glass. This is not a design that can be worked with at close range. It must be seen from a distance. That way, alignments, pairings, or directions that create stops in the even movement of the elements over the surface become obvious at once.

Figure 2-20 shows a well-resolved surface in

FIGURE 2–20
Distribution—good example of basic game.

which all parts are in controlled movement. There is no apparent repetition in the position of the lines. Compare it to Figure 2-21, in which the linear elements are pushed too close together in some areas, and begin to group and create visual pauses on the surface. Along the top row of grid units, three horizontals form a counterdirection to the vertically placed lines that negate the idea of evenness. Again on the top row, the inverted V-shape reflects the V-shape on the bottom, making a connection across the surface that is out of context with it. This surface is not a good example, but it is useful in that it shows many of the things to be avoided if one wants to meet the criterion of a smooth flow of countermovements within the arrangement of the design elements on the grid foundation.

No doubt there will always be some minor areas that do not satisfy the designer completely, but rather than dwell on them it is better to go on to another surface, correcting through a series of plates—each built on the experience of the last one—rather than laboring too long over a single plate. After you have done four or five surfaces and have grasped the idea, the size of the total area should be increased and the game started again. Increase the grid from 64 to 144 units to set up a more difficult problem. A very good solution is shown in Figure 2-22. The few weak areas in it are successfully absorbed into the great vitality of the overall surface.

GAME B
OPPOSITIONS:
USING CONTRASTS

Once the surfaces are completed in their skeletal form, the structures may be used for extensions using varied elements to produce a series of related surfaces, each with its own particular characteristics, but all relating to the same thematic idea: contained and continuous movement over the surface. For example, a thick bar can be used to give a heavier, more emphatic reading, larger in scale, or it can be broken to create a secondary interest, such as that shown in Figure 2-23.

Oppositions can be played by varying and increasing the design elements so that they become very contrasting to each other and re-form when combined to give another character to the surface. Figure 2-24 shows a bar that has been broken by an opposing smaller line. The articulation at the join creates a counterelement subordinate in size and opposed to the direction of the major design elements. Another opposition is shown in Figure 2-25, in which the surface is composed of both thick and thin lines, distributed on a checkerboard layout, which appears to create two surfaces, one above and one below, in the surface plane. Notice that in all the examples the basic distribution shown in Figure 2-20 could be used as a

FIGURE 2–21
Distribution—bad example of basic game.

FIGURE 2–22
Distribution, expanded size. Student project
by Susan D. Thomas, designer.

FIGURE 2–23
Broken line.

FIGURE 2–25
Thick and thin lines.

FIGURE 2–24
Opposed line.

basis for the extensions, although as the elements change in character they may need adjusting to accommodate the new factors introduced into the design by the variations.

Also, just as a straight line may be used, so may a curved line, as shown in Figure 2-26, and used in any of the ways discussed above. The character of curved lines combined with a right-angled grid structure often produces interesting effects that are not possible to get using only straight lines. Used singly, as thick and thin, or in other combinations, the shapes have a unique quality that is quite different from that of the preceding examples.

Although using a straight line at a 90° angle to any of the sides of the grid unit has limitations not encountered when using angled or curved lines, creating a distributed surface with such a design element is entirely possible, although the results will probably be less interesting than the others. The surfaces will appear less active, with movements that are more those of stress and release rather than flow. Using acute or obtuse angles allows considerable variety in position, which is limited by using a 90° angle, and the work moves very slowly since so many alternatives have to be tried out before a satisfactory non-repeating surface is obtained. Nevertheless, the effort is rewarded by the different kind of surface shown in Figure 2-27, and it is an excellent discipline in seeing and controlling the interactions of the design units.

DISTRIBUTION

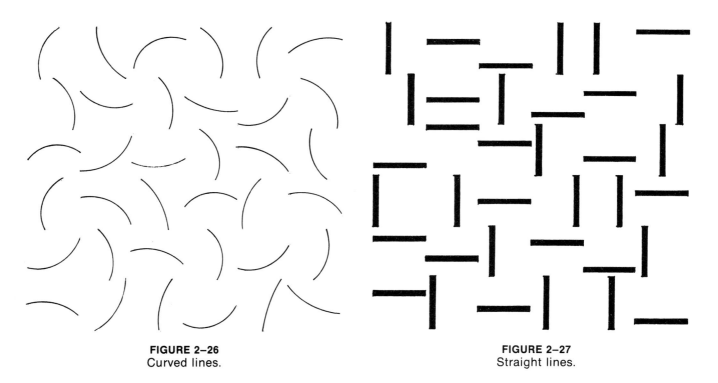

FIGURE 2–26
Curved lines.

FIGURE 2–27
Straight lines.

LINE AS SHAPE AXIS

Either a staright or a curved line may be used as an axis for other shapes. For example, a straight line can become the center, or controlling line, for a small scale planar shape—its spine, so to speak. A curved line makes an ideal axis for developing organic shapes based on models from nature. On the worksheet, Figure 2-28, a leaf-like shape based on a curved line is shown along with other shape possibilities based on straight or curved axes. Many other kinds of organic shapes, either pictorial or abstract can be developed, but in all of them the integration of the surface elements and the total effect of the completed surface are always more important than any attempt at a literal depiction of a subject. Shapes should always be based on the exchange of dark and light in the design units, as was discussed in the Introduction.

EXTENDING THE GAME

It is necessary for the serious student to take the materials developed from the basic games and work them through a series of self-structured exercises. If ideas occur while working—and they will—they should be tried out and the connections to basic forms should be made. In this way, by working and thinking and

inventing—by extending beyond the taught materials—versatility and confidence are gained. Look back over the examples and compare them for their correspondences and distinctions; by comparison, from example to example, and then by referring back to Pattern structures, the visual point and purpose of the method can be clarified and made self-explanatory, and a full visual definition of the differences between the structures can be seen.

THE DOT

The last in the sequence of primary elements, which includes plane and line, is the dot—the simplest element in surface design. Sometimes seen as the beginning of a line, sometimes as the beginning of a logical sequence from dot extended to line, and line extended to plane, a dot—or point—is a staple pattern element.

No single design element really exists in isolation—just of or by itself—and design elements usually imply other design elements: plane next to plane creates a new plane, or a line, for example. Dots, when placed over a surface, connect with each other as one's eye moves from point to point, drawing invisible connecting lines between them, or follows their movements when they are grouped on the surface, as shown in Figure 2-8.

A single dot on a supporting field is a point of

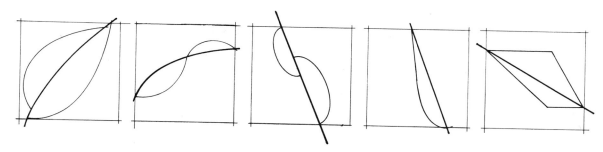

FIGURE 2–28
Lines as axes for other shapes.

concentration that defines the field, but when many dots are placed over a surface a web of connections is created which parallels the activity of line and plane seen in the preceding examples of distributed surfaces. Placing dots on the grid is another basic Distribution game, identical in purpose to the example played with lines shown in Figure 2-20. All the procedures are the same, except that a dot is used as the design element, with its position continually varied within the grid units, as shown in Figure 2-29. Several variations suggest themselves. For example, a different kind of surface can be created by increasing the size of the dot. This raises a question. When does a dot (which does not have to be circular in shape) become a plane? The decision is made by letting the ground, whether it be black or white, be clearly dominant in area, as it was

with line. Another interesting variation can be made by combining two sizes of dots, which is similiar to combining thick and thin lines, shown in Figure 2-25. As in that example, greater control of the surface is gained if the grid is handled as a checkerboard, with large and small elements arranged on alternating units, as shown in Figure 2-30. And it is certainly possible to combine large and small dots within one grid unit as another variation.

A dot may be used as the center of a more complex shape, as a line can be used as an axis for organizing new shapes. The structure developed from playing the game with this design element should be considered as another basic diagram, and used as a foundation for as many different surfaces as the individual designer chooses to develop.

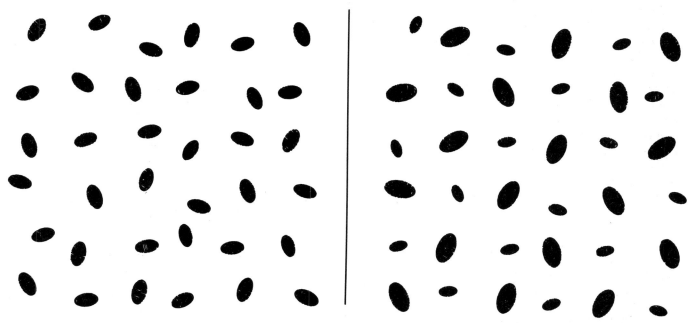

FIGURE 2–29
Small dots.

FIGURE 2–30
Large and small dots.

MAKING A REPEAT

Any surface produced so far in Distribution can be used as a continuous repeat for a printed length of cloth or paper, or some other design application where an all-over surface is needed. A properly constructed square should combine with itself in length or breadth without break, and that is the simplest method of repeat. However, it is difficult to calculate exactly how the four edges will relate and whether or not alignments or pairings will become apparent when the area is repeated. A simple way to check this is shown in the accompanying diagrams, Figures 2-31 and 2-32, which can also be used to make an area that will repeat exactly with itself.

First, cut the square design into four exactly equal smaller squares on the center horizontal and center vertical grid lines. Then reverse the positions of the square diagonally. That is, lower right is moved to upper left, upper left to lower right. In the same way, upper right becomes lower left, and vice versa. The new arrangement is shown diagrammatically in Figure 2-32. Any adjustments in distribution that have to be made are done within the body of the re-formed square, but none should be necessary at the edges which will join and re-form the original configuration at top, bottom, and sides, when the entire area is put into register and repeated. This new square can be repeated *ad infinitum* in a horizontal or vertical direction, or both, to make a continuous surface.

GAME C
COMBINATIONS

"Leaf and Flower Forms," the *kata-gami* shown in Figure 2-33, is a remarkable combination of sharply angled planes and curvilinear organic shapes. Its basic layout is similiar to the patchwork quilt shown in Figure 2-4, but it presents a clearer surface while being more complex in organization than that example. The main difference is the integration of opposing curves and angles in the stencil; the quilt uses each patch as a separate field for some added figurative interest. The quilt is meant to be seen and used as a complete object; the *kata-gami* is one part of a larger design. Each is a good study example of Distribution, contrasting as the pieces are in origin, technique, and application, but closely related in combining many irregular shapes to make one consistent field.

Neither the design of the stencil nor the quilt is

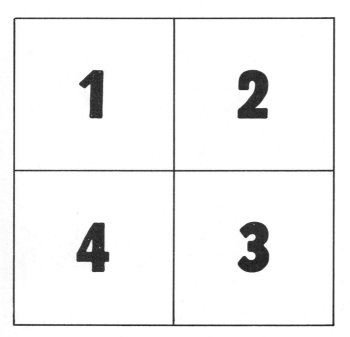

FIGURE 2–31
How to make a repeat.

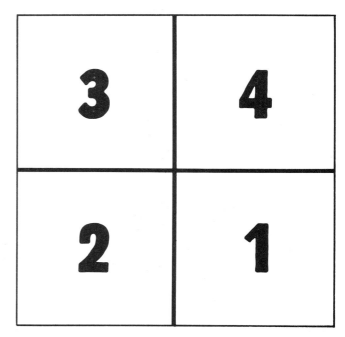

FIGURE 2–32
How to make a repeat.

organized on a grid, as is the stencil shown in Figure 2-1 and the quilt shown in Figure 2-3. Like many of the *kata-gami* shown, the Leaf and Flower stencil is one unit of a design meant to be realized by repetition. It is shown for its imaginative combination of graphic elements and as a context within which to describe a new game: *Combinations*—putting together things that say little by themselves, but when joined create fresh, unexpected effects. The stencil's controlling plane is an assemblage of angled shapes figured with minute patterns that read as visual grays. They are combined with contrasting subordinate lines of organic shapes that are seen through the patterns, reinterpreting them on many levels within the various surface planes. It is the combination of the two that is exciting; whatever interest the separate parts might have is not equal to the visual interest created when they are joined into a new surface.

FIGURE 2–33
Kata-gami: Leaf and Flower Forms.
Courtesy of The Seattle Art Museum, Eugene Fuller
Memorial Collection.

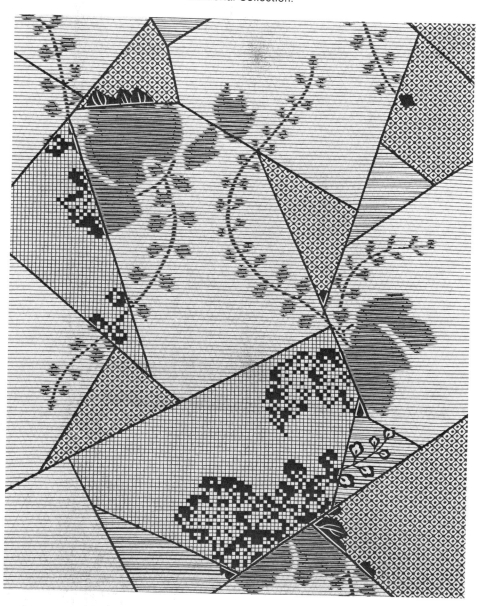

Any all-over arrangement of dots or lines created by Distribution can stand as it is, and may prove to be a handsome example, but once the problem of even distribution of the elements has been solved, the basic purpose of the game has been satisfied. To continue doing the same thing would only produce a pointless series of dry surfaces. A better idea is to use them as foundations for other kinds of shape invention—as already suggested—or to extend the design possibilities by combining surfaces of a different character, which is suggested by the stencil.

FIRST MOVES

To play Combinations, return to the grid foundation. Select two contrasting completed surfaces as models. It is not possible, except by coincidence, to place one surface on top of the other and immediately have a combination that will make visual sense. The grid and the surfaces chosen have to be worked together through new relationships using the methods described for the basic game in Distribution to produce a surface that is an integration of the composing elements. A minimal diagram of combined dots and lines is given in Figure 2-34 to suggest one way of starting. The diagram immediately suggests that some changes would make the surface more interesting: increasing

or decreasing the scale of the dots or the lines, or incorporating a curved line, for example. Or, to return to the model of the *kata-gami*, the dots could be distributed as a countermovement to the all-over distribution of the lines. And so on. Possible combinations are limited only by one's imaginative comprehension of the structures involved.

INTERPRETING MODELS

One design is rarely, if ever, complete in itself in the designer's work sequence. It may stand as a self-contained finished piece, but it is also a continuation of previous work, and a source for new designs. By looking at a finished surface of distributed straight or curved lines as a new kind of grid foundation, or looking at it in combination with the regular right-angled grid, and considering that as a basis for design development rather than finished work, another range of design extensions opens up. For example, by using the lines of the surface shown in Figure 2-20 as edges of shapes made from their interplay with the basic grid, a new design structure is defined. One of the several ways in which the structure can be interpreted is diagrammed in Figure 2-35, using visual grays.

Using still another stencil as a point of departure, the swelling shapes of "Water Pattern," Figure 2-36,

FIGURE 2—34
Combinations—dots and lines.

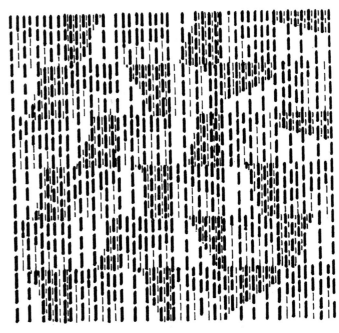

FIGURE 2—35
Shapes from Figure 2—20 and basic grid.

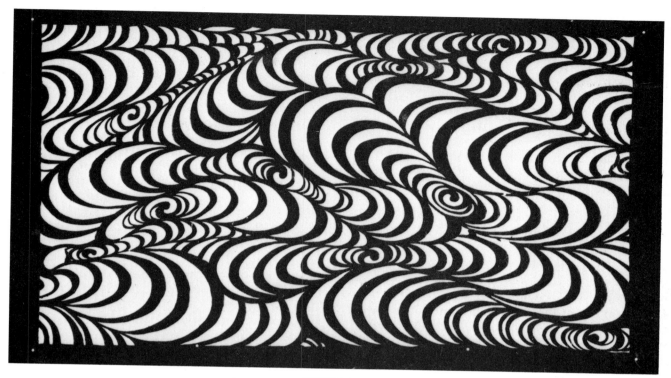

FIGURE 2–36
Kata-gami: Water Pattern. 19 × 34.2 cm.
Courtesy of Cooper-Hewitt Museum, The Smithsonian Institution's
National Museum of Design.

provide the source for the design units shown in Figure 2-37. The linear elements have been freely translated from the original surface and used on a structure similar to that of Figure 2-35. The difference is that the figured areas have been confined to the contained grid unit, subdivided by an angled line.

"Water Patterns" is a good model. It is simple in basic organization, uses a minimum of graphic means, and maintains very active but contained movements on the surface—all of which are the integral parts of the definition of Distribution. Like "Leaf and Flower Forms" (Figure 2-33), it is planned as a single unit that is meant to be repeated, but both examples are worth studying as self-contained design for their coherent, clearly defined relationships, as well as for a comparison of the contrasts and correspondences in the way the two surfaces are put together. Copying them, unless it is done to analyze organization, does not serve a valid purpose, but interpretation involves understanding what is being interpreted, and as such can be a source of original ideas. It makes a wide variety of designs accessible as models for further work by clarifying the common connections between what may at first appear as several dissimiliar surfaces.

FIGURE 2–37
Surface developed from Figure 2–36.

87

The painted bark cloth shown in Figure 2-38, for example, certainly does not fit the definition of Distribution. It is a checkerboard-based pattern, combining asymmetrical design units with alternating units of centrally placed large dots. This is a worthwhile study piece for the interplay of dot, line, and plane, combined in a handsome, sturdy design, bordered at the bottom by an intricately worked compound stripe. The symmetrical and asymmetrical areas contain design materials that can be used for interpretations in a combination of Pattern and Distribution forms.

Such a design is shown in Figure 2-39. It is based on a foundation of a diagonal stripe—Figure 1-31 from Pattern—which is suggested by the diagonals in the asymmetrical units, and combined with an arrangement of distributed lines taken from Figure 2-20. Using dark-light and a distribution of dots—again taken from the model—the involved surface shown in the figure was developed. This shows only one possibility of many that could be created on the basis of the design elements used in the bark cloth.

DESIGN ANALYSIS

At this point the first illustration, Figure 2-1, can be analyzed and its method of organization easily approximated by using the surface in Figure 2-26 as a foundation diagram. By carefully controlling the entire surface distribution, it is possible to extend linear elements beyond the limitation of a single grid unit and let them reach into adjoining grid units. If the lines are then combined with distributed dots, an abstraction of a single repeat unit of the stencil emerges, as shown in Figure 2-40. This, in turn, can become a foundation for a new series of designs.

The work is cumulative. By reviewing one's own work, re-interpreting it as a model for more work, or discovering new models that suggest other ways of reworking or extending the foundations of the basic games in Distribution, new insights into existing forms can be gained. They can be seen from different standpoints, varied in application, and synthesized in new designs—all of which is the purpose of playing Combinations.

FIGURE 2–38
Painted bark cloth.
Courtesy of the University of British Columbia Museum of Anthropology.

FIGURE 2–39
Surface developed from Figure 2–38.

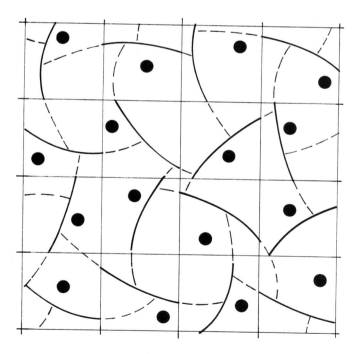

FIGURE 2–40
Reconstruction of Figure 2–1, Leafy Vine.

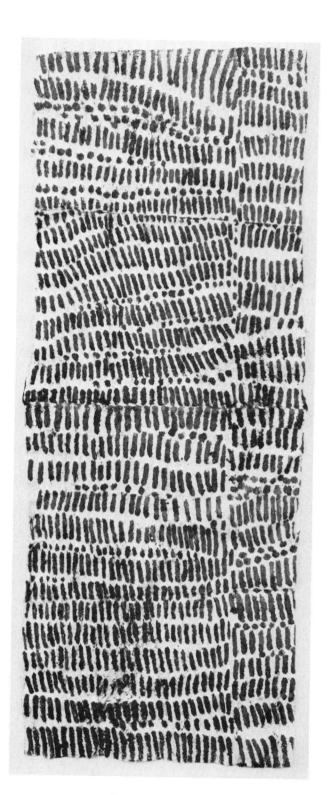

FIGURE 2–41
Beaten bark cloth, painted.
Pygmy, Ituri forest. Republic of Zaïre.
Courtesy, Field Museum of National History, Chicago.

COMPOSITION

UNEQUAL MOVEMENT
OF UNEQUAL ELEMENTS
OVER THE SURFACE

FIGURE 3–1
The Hundred Black Crows. Japanese Six-fold screen,
early 17th century.
Courtesy of The Seattle Art Museum, Eugene Fuller
Memorial Collection.

As we saw in Chapters 1 and 2, the movements in Pattern and Distribution are multiple and equal. Equal Pattern elements and unequal Distribution elements require different kinds of rhythmic arrangements to develop intact surfaces; however, in both, the fundamental rhythm is that of a simple repeat. Countermovement is a different kind of rhythm than simple repetition, but that rhythm is its basis, since a contrast works only in terms of the thing to which it is contrasted, just as a dancer is free to move with or against the beat.

Composition, on the other hand, deals with equalizing, or unifying, disparate design elements and contrasting movements within a correlating rhythmic framework that is more complex than uniform repetition. Units may not repeat exactly, elements may contrast, and many movements may combine in a single movement. These differences are harmonized in the rhythmic relationships established between them, synthesizing a variety of separate impressions into a single surface. There is an assumption when composing that there is something that wants to be composed and that it wants to be composed for a reason. The "something" is usually a number of images or elements, and the "reason" is to discover by organization the form the elements will reveal when brought together. Any random assemblage of shapes or objects could qualify as a composition of a kind, but if the creator or the observer is bothered or dissatisfied with the result (allowing for pleasant or unpleasant emotional reactions to the particular subject matter of the hypothetical composition) that reaction will probably be based on the relation of the parts of the composition as they fail to complete themselves into a comprehensible whole. In the broadest sense, then, a composition is many things occurring simultaneously in one thing, and comprehended as a whole through the relationships between them. These relationships, or connections, are the structure of the composition, and their relational order is the reason for the composition: it yields form.

PATTERN AS BASIS

Everyone is concerned with composition in one way or another whenever he tries to make sense of something. Composition can be thought about, worked with, seen as good or bad in example, but it can never be complete. It is always continuing to develop in one's work. Methods and results are continually being questioned and new ways being planned. The search for the appropriate vocabulary of visual elements suitable for the needs of individual expression, and for the structures that will organize them, and the techniques to give the ideas their finished form, is continual. Consequently, almost any point is a point of departure for a discussion of composition that will lead immediately to another connected point and still another, until the connections make a web in which each point seems to be of equal importance. Nothing can be considered without everything being considered. But an initial move, gesture, or statement must be made; something must be started if understanding is to be unravelled from the web of connections. Here, pattern forms are utilized as a foundation for composition. The connections are sequential: from the rhythm of single units arranged in equal movements (Pattern), through the manipulation of that rhythmic basis (Distribution), to the many possible arrangements of contrasting elements in complex rhythmic combinations (Composition).

Composition is about methods of organization developed in Pattern and Distribution, and the search for organization in a composition is a search for its pattern base. We are left, then, not with one way of making a composition, but with many possible ways, and the games in this chapter are played to discover some of them.

FIRST MOVES

An equal dark-light exchange is combined with a symmetrical curve to make the simple pattern statement shown in Figure 3-2. Short diagonal movements play against the dominant organization of a stripe made up of reversed units in an evenly balanced rhythm typical of pattern. One manipulation of the design unit is shown in Figure 3-3. In it, the subordinate diagonal movement of the first example has become the dominant movement, nearly absorbing the contrasting verticals in a strong movement from left to right. Each movement—vertical or diagonal—is evolved from the manipulation of the design unit; it is a result of placing the units in different positions, then repeating them as pattern.

91

COMPOSITION

FIGURE 3–2   **FIGURE 3–3**
Two student projects on Pattern, by Jim Cameron, designer.

The movement in the second pattern is akin to the movement used to organize "The Hundred Black Crows" (Figure 3-1), one of a pair of six-fold screens painted in Japan in the 17th century. (Its companion screen is shown in Figure 3-6.) Two groups of crows are arranged over the horizontal surface, one flying, the other on the ground. Their line of movement is paralleled by repeating short diagonals throughout the lower group of birds on the ground, creating one continuous dominant movement across the six panels of the screen, from upper left to lower right. Other birds fly against the movement of those at the left, or are placed in opposing positions to those on the ground.

DOMINANT AND SUBORDINATE MOVEMENT

The consistency of shape, which is pattern-like, and the interplay of a strong controlling movement, and subordinate countermovements, have a basic similiarity to the same factors used in the patterned surface shown in Figure 3-3. The way in which the movement is established is different, however. The diagonal movement in the pattern is a product of manipulation, whereas the movement in the screen appears to be carefully planned beforehand.

DIFFERENCES BETWEEN PATTERN, DISTRIBUTION, AND COMPOSITION

The design of the screen introduces a primary distinction between Pattern, Distribution, and Composition, and shows one way of ordering a surface. There are other basic methods that should be discussed in preparation for the games in Composition. For example, the lines incised on the surface of the Baluba mask from the Republic of Zaïre, shown in Figure 3-4, move inward in equally spaced curves to the eyes; a reverse chevron extends the join above the nose to its tip; four straight lines are drawn on the upper lip of the rectangular mouth. Curved, angled, and straight lines are combined in a decreasing order of importance. The design is made up of like elements that do not repeat metrically as in pattern, nor are they evenly distributed. The mask is a powerful, unified, symmetrical design, focussed on the plain surfaces of the sleepy-looking eyes. It divides into two equal halves along a central axis and converges to a point on that axis. It is dominantly round, with nose and mouth contrasted subordinately to the defining roundness. It is composed of symmetrical curvilinear rhythms.

Another example is "Deer and Poems," painted during the Edo period (17th century) by the Japanese artist Sotatsu. This is a narrow handscroll only $12\frac{1}{2}$

FIGURE 3–4
Round mask. Baluba, Republic of Zaïre.
Courtesy of The Buffalo Museum of Science.

inches wide and just over 30 feet long. Such scrolls were usually planned to be looked at sections at a time, so the detail shown in Figure 3-5 can merely begin to capture the lyrical quality of the whole painting.

Few graphic elements are used in the painting and they are simple: washes of value, straight and curved lines, and dots. The shape and position of each deer varies from that of every other deer, but the consistent drawing of their forms—particularly in the strong back and breast curves—sets up a strong repetitive rhythm, nicely countered by the straight lines of the animals' legs. The composition flows out of the massed forms on the right, moves upward, and curves in a long sweeping movement accentuated by the forward, then upward, then downward positions of the heads. This section of the total composition centers on the diagonally placed masses that move upward from right to left. The movement is emphasized by

the contrasting straight lines of the legs, and the grouped darks which are framed by light forms that weave through the composition.

The mask and scroll are objects different in kind, origin, and purpose, but they share a similiar visual vocabulary of simple shapes and curved lines, and each combines them with strong clear movements into symmetrical and asymmetrical organizations. The lines of the mask move steadily to and from its center; the deer around a curve with a dominant upward movement. The question is, are the movements drawn from the arrangements, or are the movements established as a control for the arrangements? The answer is the latter: the movement—symmetrical and centered, or asymmetrical and uncentered—organizes the repetition of similiar design elements into rhythms different in effect than those of Pattern or Distribution.

FIGURE 3–5
Deer Scroll.
Courtesy of The Seattle Art Museum,
Gift of Mrs. Donald E. Frederick.

CENTERING

Figure 3-6 is the companion piece to the Japanese screen "The Hundred Black Crows" (Figure 3-1). The crows are in silhouette—in contrast to the line and wash rendering of the scroll—but their shapes are as insistently repetitive as those of the deer. The paintings are organized in different ways. Essentially, there is one group of figures and one dominant movement in the "Deer and Poems" handscroll, in contrast to the crows which are arranged in three related groups that center on the pair of squabbling birds. The two lower groups are organized in an undulating movement that runs the length of the screen, each with its own center, and the upper group is contained within a wide, slightly flattened semi-circle, so that one's eye

FIGURE 3–6
The Hundred Black Crows.
Courtesy of The Seattle Art Museum, Eugene Fuller
Memorial Collection.

goes from group to group to gain the sense of the composition, rather than being taken along the single curving movement that terminates in the upper left of the handscroll. Although the confronted birds do create a visual center in the composition—the crow's tailfeathers point downward to the lower groups, and the open beaks of the birds on the ground point upward to them, and the pairs' wings are extended to join the upper group—it acts more as a pivot for the vigorous actions on the screen panels. This is a different kind of centering than the deliberate dead-center shown in the Baluba mask.

Some mention must be made of the use of open space in the two compositions. In neither is it merely empty space, but space carefully shaped by the placement of the figures on the scroll and screen. On the scroll it is shaped as a curve which echoes the arrangement of the deer in a reverse shape that swells up and moves down in correspondence to the long controlling curve, reinforcing its definition. On the screen it has a long shape that diminishes in size as it moves from left to right, delineated by groups of birds. There is an interesting exchange of dark and light eccentric shapes created by the juxtaposition of the silhouettes of the birds within each group. This kind of "making all the spaces work" is a direct extension of the inclusive thinking behind the methods used when making a design unit that will combine with itself to make new shapes when put into repeat.

surface organization is clear, check it often by looking at it from a distance, or use a reducing glass, while the work is in progress.

FIRST MOVES

The simplest way of playing Transitions is to devise a method of moving through a sequence of sizes using a consistent design unit, but varying its proportion, as shown in Figure 3-7. The amounts of dark and light exchange evenly, dark areas increasing within the same ratio as the units move upward, or vice versa as they move downward. The transitional movement is established on a diagonal running from lower left to upper right across the grid. A nearly equal and opposite movement to the diagonal is created on the long sides of the triangles. The design unit is the same dark-light combination of triangles used for Pattern games, but this format can be used with other geometric shapes—different triangles, segments of circles, rectangles, or variations on these shapes—for further experimentation.

The second example, Figure 3-8, is more complex than the first since it deals with a transition of shape and size rather than with size only, as in the preceding example. Reading the surface from the upper left of the grid to the lower right, one is aware of a very gradual transformation of the light quarter-

GAME A
TRANSITIONS:
CONTROLLING MOVEMENT

The first game in Composition puts into practice the idea of organizing a surface by creating a single unifying rhythm through the movement of the design elements, rather than the many movements of Distribution, or the repetition of Pattern. Five possible ways of playing the game will produce different effects on the surface, as shown in the following examples. They are not meant to be seen as finished pieces, but as some bases for individual interpretation. Cut and paste, drawing with felt-tipped pen, or any of the working methods used for the other games may be used to play Transitions. The point of the game is to create a dominant movement over the surface; any contrasting movements that may appear in the design should be of subordinate importance. To make sure that the

FIGURE 3–7
Transitions—proportionate triangle.

COMPOSITION

FIGURE 3–8
Transitions—shape change.

FIGURE 3–9
Transitions.

circle as it appears to increase and flatten in its exchange with the dark shapes. At the center, the field transposes and the dark and light positions are reversed. It is the strong diagonal line of transition that organizes the surface. Besides curved to angled, try playing this version of the game by moving from square to round, round to triangular, or triangular to square.

The third example, Figure 3-9, takes its organization from Distribution and combines it with the idea of interchanging sizes, shown in Figure 3-7, in still another strong diagonal surface movement. Figure 3-10 shows one more adaptation of a Distribution format, joined with the reversal suggested in Figure 3-8, but uses contrasting shapes as well as amounts. Additional combinations may be drawn from Pattern and Distribution work and used to play other variations of Transitions.

The fifth example, Figure 3-11, diagrams two suggestions for organizing contrasting movements within a dominant vertical movement on the surface. You can move either from straight to angled, or from straight to curved, using lines of consistent width, or with an increasing-decreasing ratio of thicknesses, or with lines that transpose to planes.

Remember that a transition is like an edge: it separates and joins at the same time. When playing all versions of the game concentrate on creating an even transition *through* the elements used, so that the

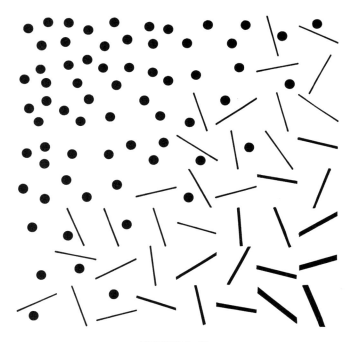

FIGURE 3–10
Transitions.

GAME A: TRANSITIONS

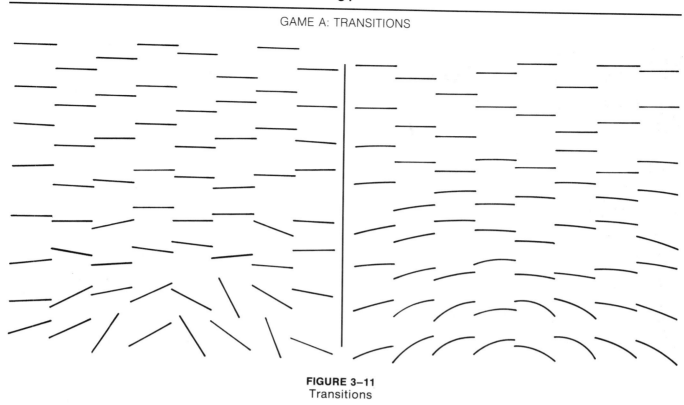

FIGURE 3–11
Transitions

contrasts are joined in one continuous movement and do not stand out or separate from the surface as a whole. It will take time and a considerable amount of visual juggling to arrive at a satisfying order of design elements, and the process is not unlike that used to play Distribution, which is the basis of the game. The results of playing will be several surfaces that can be used either as design units and repeated for an all-over continuous surface, or by themselves as simple single composed areas, or—and most important—as foundations for more complex and subtle kinds of transitions, such as those shown in the following examples.

DESIGN ANALYSIS

In the photograph shown in Figure 3-12, the composition can be read as a transition from the upper straight lines through the regular curve of the plate edge to the irregular curve of the eggs, with the small triangular dot between them acting as a visual period to the arrangement. Or, it can be read in reverse: as an expansion from the same dot through a series of increasingly relaxed curves that become straight lines. Either way, the contrast of straight and curved shapes creates tension, and consequently visual interest, in the photograph. The linear organization is strong in

repetition and variation, and the plate edge decorated with half circles is an effective joining of straight and curved into a clear rhythmic order. What might remain as visually ambiguous areas in the lower part of the composition are explained and clarified in the context of the whole and add further interest when contrasted with the other elements in the composition. The subject matter—eggs on a plate—seems incidental to the organization of the entire area. The combination of straight, curved, and round, the movement through this sequence, the containment of the egg shapes, the variations in line, and the way in which all of these elements are put together are more important in the total visual impression. The organization of the composition has little to do with the associations that may be connected to the objects used as subject matter. The composition is about transition.

The final illustration in this sequence, Figure 3-13, is of a relief print on paper by the contemporary Japanese artist Masakatsu Ueda. It is a centered composition using only dots to create a subtle, equivocal image of interplay. Dots transpose from large to small as they move toward the center in a steady rhythm. A reverse transition, from small to large, is superimposed on this progressive rhythm, moves through it, and joins it in contiguous circles at the center. Visually, it is an intriguing union of contrasting sizes and opposed amounts.

COMPOSITION

FIGURE 3–12
Photograph, by Shinya Uno.

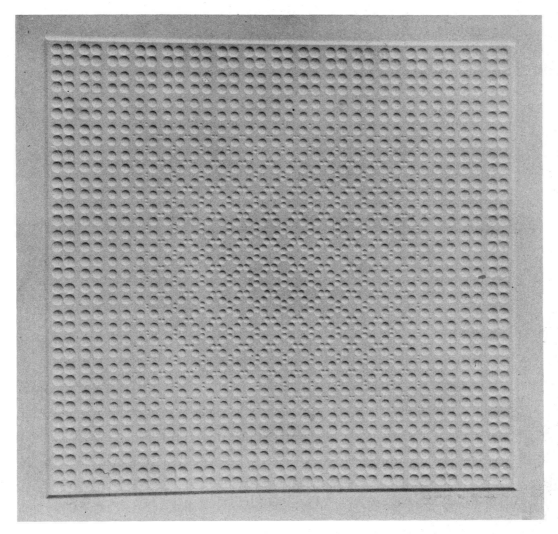

FIGURE 3–13
Masakatsu Ueda, Relief print No. 17 (1971).

RHYTHMIC BALANCE

Learning to control the movements between elements to create a dominant movement is learning to control one important part of composition while at the same time defining the differences between the movements of Pattern or Distribution, and the movements of Composition. Another difference between Pattern, Distribution, and Composition games is the manner in which design units join. All the games are played on a grid—it is the common basis of the three methods of organization. But, just as two design elements join to make a new element—the compound unit of Pattern or Distribution—further manipulation of the design units make still more complex combinations. These are groups, or clusters, which are drawn out of the foundation of the regular patterned surface. Although composed of smaller joined units equal in size, they combine in interacting areas of dark and light of unequal weight balanced by controlling their movements. Another difference is that the new shapes are non-repeating, and can be arranged over the surface either symmetrically or asymmetrically. The balance of complex rhythms takes dominance over simple repetition as organization, and the static one-to-one relationships of Pattern become visually subordinate within the finished surface.

Figure 3-14 shows an arrangement of such shapes. Large and small triangles, parallelograms, hooked shapes, obtuse and acute angles, all are combined in a single composition. All of the shapes are made up, in one combination or another, of the basic design unit: right-angled dark-light triangles. The dominant movement of the composition is a revolution around the centrally placed light parallelogram. Although there is considerable angular movement within the field, the movements counter one another and the area remains contained except for the arrow-shape in the upper right-hand corner which appears to point out of the field and disrupts the otherwise balanced asymmetrical distribution of dark-light masses. Generally, however, throughout the piece there is a successful variation of related shapes composed of joined triangles as the dark-light areas merge to create mutually defining shapes—the basic concept of the first moves of Pattern games. Also, the continual and contained movement of the elements, and the arrangement of larger and smaller shapes that do not repeat, connect directly to the surface organization explored in Distribution. The composition, rather than being imposed upon the surface, is drawn out of it by manipulating the basic design element to make a series of individual shapes distributed around a center in a succession of sharp-angled movements. Although the graphic elements and the working methods

of Pattern and Distribution games are used in part, the result is neither, but a self-contained composed unit. It is a good example of the use of simple pattern elements joined together in rhythmic variations to produce complex results.

Movement does not necessarily imply an even flow of elements nor an unbroken continuity of impressions. It can be used that way, and it is, in the "Deer and Poems" handscroll, the photograph, and the relief print. It is not used that way in the Baluba mask nor in the dark-light study of Figure 3-14. The mask and the print are symmetrical, but they are not identical symmetrical organizations; their movements are contrasting. Movement is an expression of rhythm, and the contrasting rhythms of the mask and the relief print have been described. The dark-light composition hardly flows; it moves in sharp increments to its center. The mask and relief print, too, are centered, but the comparison between them and the black and white study is one of symmetrical, as contrasted to asymmetrical, centering. Such differences are not as confusing as they first sound, but they cannot be made entirely clear until they are defined by example or by comparison within the context of a series of selected models, such as those we will now examine.

DESIGN ANALYSIS

Figure 3-15, a Mandingo textile from Guinea, should be compared—as an example of symmetrical composition—with the preceding illustrations and particularly with Figure 3-14. Its construction seems to be very simple, but the surface contains as many complexities as that of the dark-light study, though of a contrasting kind. Although the piece is symmetrical, it is not a mirror image layout since the position of dark and light is reversed, right and left of center—an arrangement that gives the surface a syncopation that is more interesting than an equal repeat. Six bands are aligned vertically in an arrangement that carries important cross movements in three different scales—small, medium, and large—and centers firmly in six finely scaled units which are realized in visual grays. The cross movements which integrate the contrasting sizes into equal rhythms are consistent in layout, and their boldness combined with the fineness of the central area sets up an exchange of tension in position and scale, which gives the piece its interest. A further variation on the interplay of vertical and horizontal, but in a different organization, can be seen by comparing this piece with the textile shown in Figure 3-75.

A center does not necessarily mean dead center in a composition. Another look at the illustrations

FIGURE 3–14
Composition in black and white, cut paper.

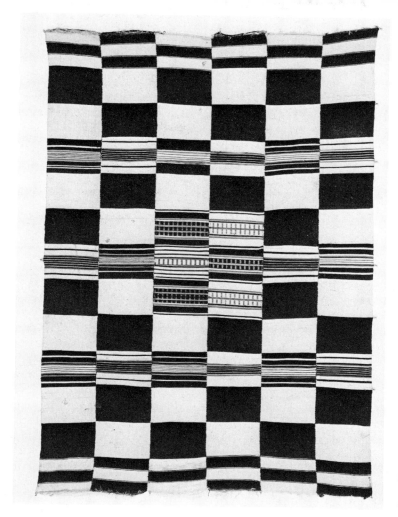

FIGURE 3–15
Men's weave. Mandingo, Guinea.
Courtesy of The American Museum
of Natural History.

should clarify this. Compare the Baluba mask with the Japanese handscroll, or the centers of the crow screens. A further comparison should be made between the mask and the Mandingo textile, both of which are symmetrical and frankly centered, and the asymmetrical dark-light composition, Figure 3-14, in which the shapes move around a center.

Another variation, in an East Indian folk embroidery, is shown in Figure 3-16. Made up of dots, lines, and whimsical human and animal shapes, the piece is composed by placing these elements on either side of a strong vertical axis which controls their arrangement. However, within that symmetrical framework there is continual variation. Few elements repeat exactly although all variations are within the symmetry of the central design which is framed, in turn, by a series of reinforcing borders. The similar size and regular placement of the many small design elements gives a first impression of even distribution centered around the fanciful anthropomorphic figure and the pair of confronted birds below it, but in fact it is a simple arrangement based upon a central-axis, mirror-image format.

FIGURE 3–16
Pakistani folk art embroidery.

101

SIMPLE EXERCISES IN BEGINNING COMPOSITION

The following two exercises have become traditional in beginning surface design classes. They are not directly connected to using pattern structures as a basis for developing compositions in two dimensions, but they are valuable small studies that call attention to movement, grouping, spacing, and edge relationships. As such, they are worth doing. Both are very simple to execute.

Figure 3-17: Use two squares of paper, one white measuring 12 × 12 inches, and the other black measuring 3 × 3 inches. Keeping the edges of the two squares parallel, place the black square on the white square in what seems to be a "best balance" position that is anyplace but center. There will be several positions that look satisfactory, but settle on one and study it. Are lengths or widths repeated? That is, when the black square divides the white square into parts, are all parts of the arrangement unequal, or are they equal in some places? Repetition of areas will tend to concentrate too much attention on themselves and negate other areas on the surface. Are all parts of the surface active? That is, does the entire page function, or do some parts seem so empty that they become visually passive? Considerable time can be spent on this exercise. The point of it is to find a position—or positions—in which the black square appears to activate the entire field so that an asymmetrical combination of dark-light areas, all of which are active, is created. The edges are considered as part of the body of the composition, as are all parts of the white ground. The figure shows one possible arrangement, but many others should be tried.

Figure 3-18: Use the same size white paper as before, and three black dots about ½ inch in diameter. Keeping in mind that the composition is to be asym-

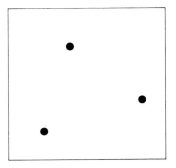

FIGURE 3–18
Dots on square.

metrical, place one dot in what seems to be a good position, and then place another dot in relation to it at a distance of five or six inches. Study the effect, and then place a third dot in relation to the others, but at a distance from them. The first dot will act as a focus, diminishing the entire page to a supporting ground. The second dot will establish a strong linear movement between it and the first dot since the human eye tends to connect points in space. The third dot will complete a triangular figure for the same reason. This figure should be studied for the effect of its position on the page with the same criteria in mind as that used in the previous exercise.

Neither of these exercises is meant to produce a finished piece of work. They are visual warm-up exercises to start thought processes flowing and to call attention to the abstract foundation of composition, regardless of the specific subject matter content. They may be elaborated by using more than one square, or a series of sizes of squares in the first, and additional dots in the second. The relationship of proportionate areas may be studied further by using a line that reaches from edge to edge, as shown in Figure 3-19;

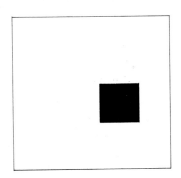

FIGURE 3–17
Square on square.

FIGURE 3–19
Line on square.

or, the three elements—dot, line, and plane—may be combined into a more complex study. In all exercises use the edges of the large plane as a guide, and keep the elements placed in it in relation to them. Otherwise the smaller elements used will tend to bunch up on the field, and the point of having all parts of the surface in action at once will be lost. Also, it is important to keep in mind that although the results of doing them may appear to be totally different from the designs done in Pattern or Distribution, they are based on the same considerations of visual order. Pattern and Distribution should be reviewed within this context so that the continuity of work is clear, and the small preliminaries look like something not put together, but belonging together.

PATTERN-BASED COMPOSITION

Everything that has been discussed to this point pertains to composition. Patterns and pattern-like distributed surfaces are particular modes of composition. And—so that nothing is wasted—those irrelevant disturbances that do not seem to be an integral part of pattern development can be used as a basis from which to discuss some elements of pattern-based composition. If Pattern establishes the basic rhythm, and Distribution varies that structure, then Composition utilizes and extends the rhythms of both of them. To follow through on the connections while elaborating on the basic exercises shown in Figures 3-17, 18, and 19, the following set of illustrations is meant to show some of these interrelations—which includes the distinctions between them.

For example, Figure 3-20 shows a pattern articulated by placing dots regularly at the intersections of a right-angled grid.

Three dots are emphasized by changing their size in Figure 3-21, and a triangular shape is drawn from the field, in the same way that a shape is established in Figure 3-18. In effect, the emphasis reduces the pattern to a supporting ground, more textured than that of Figure 3-18, but essentially passive. There is little interaction between the dot pattern and the triangle that is established by emphasizing three dots.

By subtracting two dots from the pattern, as shown in Figure 3-22, two squares are formed that are connected by a diagonal movement. Since the squares are in harmony with the square format of the example, and are multiples of the grid units, the figure seems to function in a less arbitrary manner than the triangle shown in Figure 3-21. There is a greater interaction between the pattern base and the figures drawn from it although the example does not show a complete

FIGURE 3–20
Dot sequence, articulation.

FIGURE 3–21
Dot sequence, three large dots.

composition, and the squared areas have the appearance of holes in the surface rather than an exchange of elements.

The idea of using pattern-like elements and establishing a controlling center through emphasis is shown more clearly in the ink study, Figure 3-23.

103

COMPOSITION

FIGURE 3–22
Dot sequence, subtracting two dots.

Here the rough shape toward the center right, though much the same size as the other related shapes, is given central importance by isolating it with surrounding white shapes. The white shapes diminish to lines as they are distributed towards the edges of the plane, but the black shapes maintain a consistency of size which gives greater visual interest to the composition than the simple back and forth diagonal movement in Figure 3-22. Figure 3-22 is drawn from a pattern base by interrupting the even rhythm by *subtracting* repeating elements; Figure 3-23 is drawn from distributed elements by *emphasizing* one area to destroy the evenness of the surface. Although neither idea would work to produce a consistent patterned or distributed surface, they work here as moves toward composing the surface; they are not errors but deliberate moves.

Figure 3-24 shows a complete disruption of a polka dot pattern. It is neither regular in rhythm nor even in distribution, but random, and the observer keeps moving around in it, trying to get it to cohere, which it will not. There is no visual idea to relate to in it.

At first glance, the surface shown in Figure 3-25 appears to be random, but it is not. One can draw *centers* of light from it that are contained and controlled by larger black dots that create organized transitional curvilinear movements within the surface,

FIGURE 3–23
Masses—ink study.

FIGURE 3–24
Random dots.

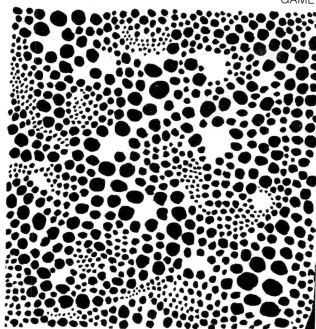

FIGURE 3–25
Dots—ink study.

FIGURE 3–26
Expanding center—ink study.

FIGURE 3–27
Diagonals—ink study.

which, in turn, are further defined and supported by the loose shapes in visual gray created by masses of smaller dots.

Figure 3-26 is another brush and ink free study on paper in which short strokes are used to form shapes that expand from and return to a *center* in the lower right of the composition. Its similarity to the preceding figure is that like marks are grouped to form large shapes, but it is different from it in shape organization. The shapes move in relation to one another in a spiral that has an ovoid shape at its center. The linear quality of the small marks produces an obvious textured quality which distinguishes it from the surface shown in Figure 3-25. But the important difference between the two surfaces, is the contrast between their basic structures.

The final example in the sequence, Figure 3-27, is more complex in its organization than any of the other surfaces shown. The combination of thick and thin brush lines creates irregular shapes—no two alike—that move from lower left to upper right with great vitality. That movement is countered and controlled by the descending movement from upper left to lower right. The piece is organized around a cross axis of *movement* that contains it on the page. There is no center as obvious as those in Figures 3-23 and 3-26, nor any use of connecting points and subordinate

COMPOSITION

movements as in Figure 3-25. Vigorous cross movement is the organizing method.

All of the brush studies use simple graphic units—dots, lines, or planes—to develop their surfaces, yet they all differ from each other in surface structure. These are the variations on the regular rhythmic structure of Pattern and Distribution that can be used as bases for Composition.

GAME B
EMPHASIS:
MANIPULATING THE SURFACE

"It all depends on where you put the emphasis" is an overworked phrase that remains as true for verbal argument as it does for visual statement. What is chosen to be forceful, or dominant in effect, on a surface conditions all subsequent relations that make a composition. There is no particular emphasis given to any one area in the Bushongo design from Africa shown in Figure 3-28. However, the dominant right-angled organization controls the many small figures used over the surface. The V-shapes and small dark areas give variety and points of concentration, but they are subordinate to the activity of the angles. Although the basic rhythm is that of the angles, it is a composition based upon the distribution of pattern-like elements, with emphasis on the rhythm of the angles.

Another aspect of emphasis, using dark and light massing and manipulation, is shown in Figures 3-29 through 3-32. These examples are meant to be seen as preliminary drawings done to explore some possibilities for composition drawn from a single patterned foundation. In the first, Figure 3-29, the repetitive structure is frankly stated and then divided in two parts diagonally, with reverse shading on the left and right sides to give contrasting surface depths.

In Figure 3-30, the elements on the left side of the composition are more elaborately manipulated to make them dominant in the composition, while the right side is developed as a patterned shape. The symmetry of the first example has given way to a combination of symmetrical and asymmetrical elements combined in one statement. Both examples depend heavily upon the horizontal banding to control them.

In the third example, Figure 3-31, the left side of the composition is as complex as that shown in the second illustration, but the right side is varied enough in itself to begin to merge with it in interest. There is less dependence upon the organizing horizontals.

In the fourth and final example in the sequence, Figure 3-32, the diagonal movement constant throughout the sequence has been maintained, but it is subordinate to the placement of five centers established by shading the round design motifs, and to the countermovements drawn from the other design

FIGURE 3–28
Bushongo design of palm cloth strips applied onto a plain
palm cloth backing. Congo-Kinshana.
From *African Designs from Traditional Sources* by Geoffrey Williams.
© 1971 Dover Publications, Inc., New York.

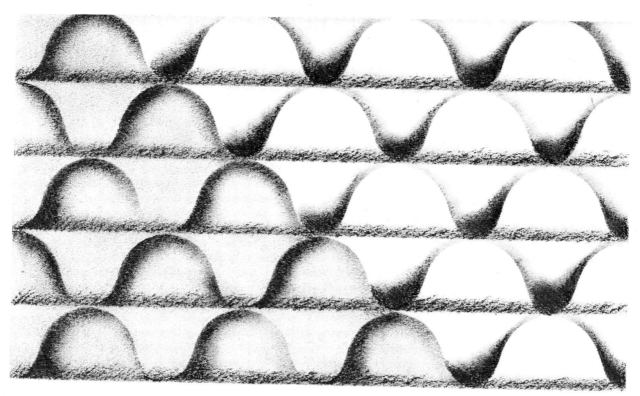

FIGURE 3–29
Drawing sequence.

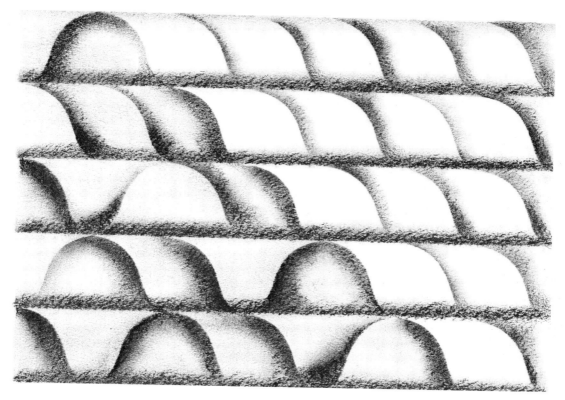

FIGURE 3–30
Drawing sequence.

107

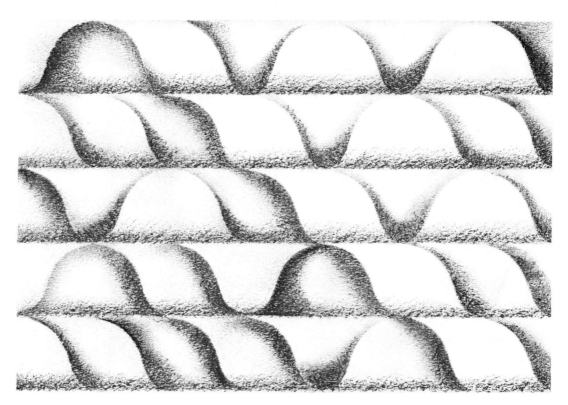

FIGURE 3–31
Drawing sequence.

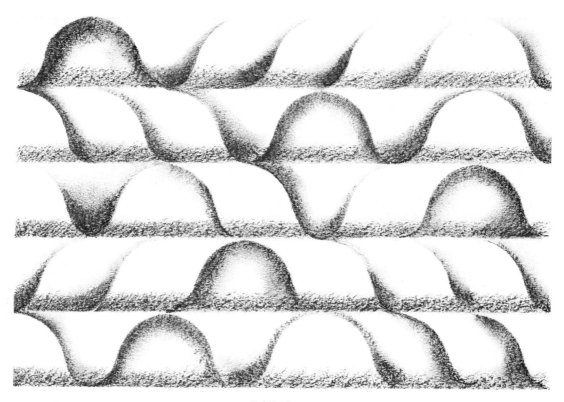

FIGURE 3–32
Drawing sequence.

elements. The method of organization is similiar to that of the dot study shown in Figure 3-25. In this example the continual interchange of surface activities begins to overcome the stolid repetition of the horizontal bands.

The sequence could be continued. For example, a next step might be to further emphasize the curvilinear diagonal movements and eliminate the horizontals as drawn lines while maintaining their order through the banded placement of the varied design elements. A step further would be to relate a drawing to the Bushongo design by emphasizing curves to create a dominant organizing rhythm, with subordinate horizontal movement. However, the examples shown are enough to illustrate the point of Emphasis and to show some of its variations.

Although most of the games in Composition can be played with dark-light only, expanding the range of materials will greatly enrich the results by making more variations in design possible. A middle value gray paper can be used, as well as a variety of visual grays. More drawing should be included, done in charcoal, Conté crayon, graphite, and felt pen. Cut and paste is still a good technique to use, but it is not the only one available, and some compatible techniques can

certainly be combined in finished pieces. Since the work here is concerned with establishing basic structures, do not use color, but work with value only.

FIRST MOVES

Emphasis, like all the games, should be considered not as an end in itself, but as a means of gaining the awareness and perception that are the starting points for further individual exploration and invention. It depends upon Pattern and Distribution for its basic materials, and the following illustrations are meant to show the complete process of developing a composition drawn from these structures.

The simple, powerful form of a Nootka Indian bird mask is shown in Figure 3-33. The general contours of the mask have been freely adapted to arrive at the basic design unit shown in Figure 3-34. No attempt has been made to transcribe the mask in detail, or be exact in its rendering. Rather, its character has been used as a point of departure to arrive at a usable shape that will combine with itself when placed within the grid units.

Three pattern manipulations of the shape are

FIGURE 3–33
Nootka Bird Mask.
Courtesy of the University of British Columbia Museum of Anthropology.

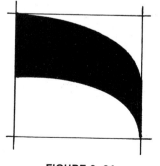

FIGURE 3–34
Nootka shape.

sketched in Figures 3-35, 3-36, and 3-37. Figure 3-37 shows the most complicated arrangement, with the line from unit to unit extended beyond the grid boundary to join the units in a series of connected curves and points.

A distributed surface is shown in Figure 3-38. By

FIGURE 3–35
Nootka straight pattern.

FIGURE 3–36
Nootka reversal.

FIGURE 3–37
Nootka rotation.

placing the design unit asymmetrically—not repeating exactly—within the successive grid units, and giving emphasis to either the upper or lower curve of the shape, a pattern-like surface is created with many movements and countermovements.

FIGURE 3–38
Nootka distribution.

DEVELOPING A COMPOSITION

Any of these surfaces can be used for developing a composition by playing Emphasis. For demonstration, the simplest—Figure 3-35—has been chosen. In order to establish dominant and subordinate areas, three values, not dark-light only, must be used, otherwise the surface will become a study in massing darks and lights, and the subtle rhythm of the pattern base will be lost.

In the first example, Figure 3-39, a centered composition is shown that has been developed in three values. First a new grid, Figure 3-40, based upon the pattern is established, and then—through emphasis—the composition is drawn from the patterned ground. Some shapes are joined to form large, dominant shapes, and others to form supporting shapes—as in the exercise shown in Figure 3-14. The areas of greatest contrast in size and value are the ones that concentrate attention.

The second composition, shown in Figure 3-41, is developed on the idea of centers. Again, the composition is based upon the grid shown in Figure 3-40 and the dominant groups drawn from the surface in much the same way as that shown in Figure 3-41.

The third composition, Figure 3-42, is based upon a strong movement over the surface.

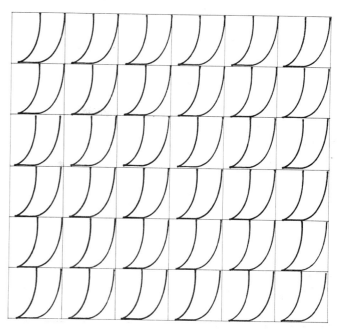

FIGURE 3–40
Nootka new grid.

After such a sequence of compositional development that has been shown on the work sheets has been gone through it should become clear that unless the basis of Pattern and Distribution has been experienced, it is difficult—if not impossible—to project ideas into compositional forms that use pattern structures as their foundation. Continual reference has to be made to the preceding work examples, and the exercises done to establish a frame of reference for the current work. From them, many extensions of the game will suggest themselves, and whatever occurs to the designer should be noted down for further individual exploration.

FIGURE 3–41
Nootka centers.

FIGURE 3–39
Nootka centered composition.

FIGURE 3–42
Nootka movement.

GAME C
LABYRINTH:
MANIPULATING THE GRID

The square design shown in Figure 3-43 is a cloth from Pakistan that has been embroidered with geometric motifs and further embellished with small rounds of mirror. The design moves from a symmetrical center through a series of borders to a bold outer edge that repeats the motif of the center. Throughout the prevailing symmetry of the surface runs a continual asymmetrical counterpoint of variations—the most obvious being in the area surrounding the center. Although it is organized as a diamond pattern, the pattern and value changes within this area give it more the appearance of a field for the central unit, rather than a border around it. There are many changes in value placement and directions used in the borders; only the outer border and inner center appear as consistent in organization, yet they too contain small variations on the pattern base.

FIGURE 3–43
Pakistani embroidered square.

This ordering in successive rows that are continually varied in design content is the model for a primary game in Composition called *Labyrinth*. It deals with four factors: (1) centered compositions, (2) consideration of the overall dynamics of the composed surface, (3) another method of drawing shapes up from the grid, and (4) a new idea, that of manipulating the grid itself. The borders of the Pakistani cloth are both separated and joined by rows of cross stitches. In Labyrinth, the idea of separate borders is replaced by the idea of a movement coiling in to the center of the page, or out from the center to the edge: it diagrams a maze leading toward a center of visual concentration.

FIRST MOVE: A NEW GRID

To play Labyrinth a new asymmetrical grid foundation based upon the right-angled grid has to be drawn. Start the game using a grid of eight by eight units and reduce it to a square of evenly spaced points at the exact intersections of the grid lines. Figure 3-44 shows the point arrangement, which will prove to be less confusing to work with than with lines. Place a piece of tracing paper over the grid. Refer to Figure 3-45 and, starting in the upper left hand corner, draw one *continuous* line—a line that remains connected to itself from grid unit to grid unit, across the top, down the

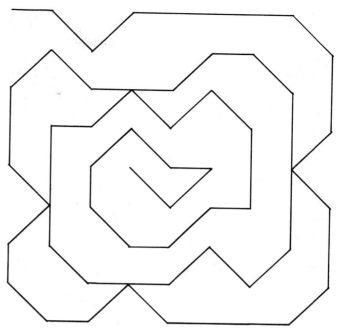

FIGURE 3–45
Labyrinth spiralling line diagram.

FIGURE 3–44
Labyrinth dot diagram.

right edge, across the bottom edge, and turns up along the left edge of the grid. At the second unit down from the top left, turn the line in and move it across the row of grid units, turning down along the right—second row in—turn in across the bottom row, and so on until the center units (there are four) are reached and the line must be terminated. The line must pass along one edge of each grid square once only, or cut diagonally across its center once only, and must remain continuous. Although this is limiting, some experimentation will show that considerable variation in arrangement is possible within that limitation. First efforts are frequently clumsy looking, but there is a positive value in the visual discipline and in the concentration and control necessary to get the entire plane to operate together at one time. If the first diagrams go wrong, discard them and begin again. Overcomplication is usually the first cause of failure, such as the result shown in Figure 3-46, which is a chaos of repeating shapes in randomly placed groups.

LINEAR MOVEMENTS

A series of shapes that have some relation to each other in their movement into the center of the plane, shown in Figure 3-45, gives a better looking result and

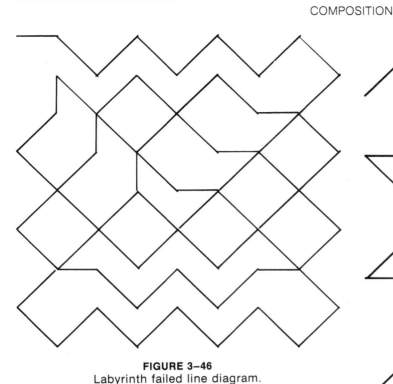

FIGURE 3–46
Labyrinth failed line diagram.

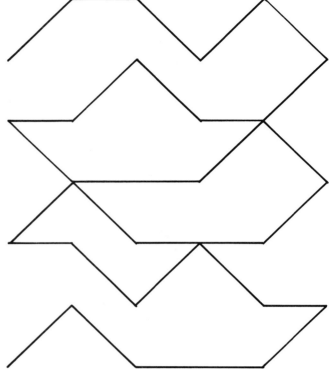

FIGURE 3–47
Labyrinth horizontal 5 × 6.

a workable diagram. The objective is to draw up, in outline, a number of angled shapes that have common boundaries, and as shown, imply a movement inward on the surface created by their placement. This will give a centered arrangement using a number of varied but related outlined shapes. The shapes are distributed around the center of the surface. Any pairings, holes in the surface, or stoppages that may happen, should be eliminated as they were in Distribution, to organize the parts of the surface into a unified whole.

Another organization based on a continuous line is that of a series of shapes arranged sequentially on the page from top to bottom. The same foundation shown in Figure 3-44 can be used, but the line is drawn from left to right on the top row, then down at an angle to the second row, across it and down at an angle to the third row, and so on until it can be ended at the final grid unit on the bottom. Such an organization is shown in Figure 3-47. The shapes do not move toward a center, but a central shape may be developed from them—central in size, or emphasis, but not necessarily centrally placed—or centers, around which the surface can be organized. Further, the example shows a variation on the size of the grid format: five units across and six units down, which gives some proportional variety to the designs; it is not necessary to adhere to a square format for everything. There is a definite horizontal banding effect in this

arrangement, which in turn may give still another effect if the surface is turned sideways and the line diagram used vertically rather than horizontally.

This kind of playing with the static grid is a game that doesn't have a specific number of moves to a conclusion that will read "Win," but sets up the possibility of using self-created visual materials as new materials, or in new ways, in a continuity that allows all preceding work to be reviewed from the standpoint of how it can be developed in different ways.

The linear diagrams show ways of manipulating the grid structure that are interesting in themselves, but they remain merely visual speculations unless some are carried to completion in dark and light. They may be used in various ways as foundations for compositions. One example, Figure 3-48, shows a dark-light arrangement based on the diagram shown in Figure 3-47, with a rather mundane composition as the result. The dark-light positions could be reversed for another effect, or both could be used in a combination—aligned side by side to make a long panel, Figure 3-49, to give a variation in the proportion of the format other than the variation suggested in Figure 3-47. Another, and perhaps more interesting variation

GAME C: LABYRINTH

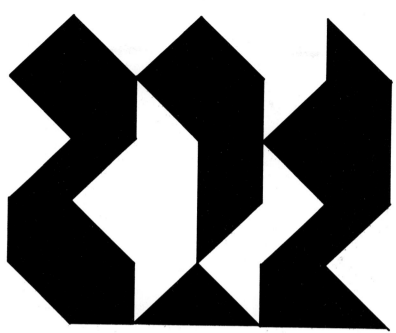

FIGURE 3–48
Labyrinth dark-light composition.

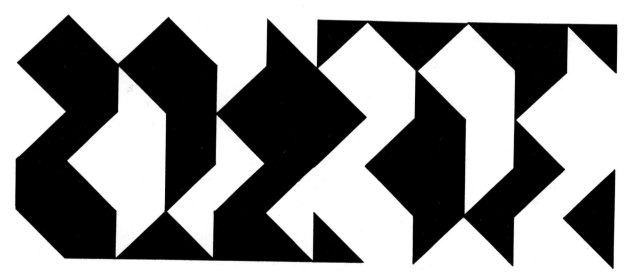

FIGURE 3–49
Labyrinth diptych on Figure 3–48.

that suggests many possibilities, is that shown in Figure 3-50, in which a pattern is created in middle values and combined with the dark-light composition.

Another approach to grid manipulation is to draw a framework from the grid using a *discontinuous* line. The composition shown in Figure 3-51 is based upon such a framework. It combines a sub-pattern of evenly spaced dots, with larger shapes arranged symmetrically on the surface. The framework is set up on the basis of using each square of the grid separately. Some are crossed with a central diagonal line, some have the line drawn on an edge, or have a straight line

FIGURE 3–50
Labyrinth pattern on Figure 3–48
in three values.

FIGURE 3–51
Labyrinth dot stencil.

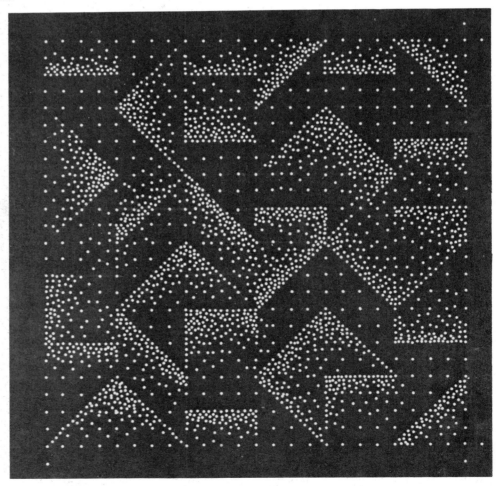

drawn across the center. The grid and the linear framework are clearly visible in the finished piece, which has been prepared as a stencil. The figures are punched into Japanese persimmon paper with a special round tool, and the repeat has been keyed on the right for registration.

Curved lines are difficult to control. They do not relate to the angles of the grid as well as straight lines do, but they can be used. A slight curve will work better than one that is very rounded. A combination of straight and curved lines is another possibility, and one that is easier to manage than just curves. Allow one line quality or the other to dominate in the first layouts, so the effects won't cancel each other out, before playing with closer proportionate relationships between the two that might produce more interesting

surface tensions of contrast. Whatever means are chosen to create the labyrinth, they must be used consistently to maintain a rhythm on the surface—one that doesn't use too many elements that are too difficult to relate to each other. The framework of Labyrinth is elaborate to begin with, and it is not necessary to use involved graphic devices to obtain a rich, varied, and interesting surface.

A single continuous curved line has been used to develop the undulating surface shown in Figure 3-52. Rather than treating each square of the grid as a separate unit (Figure 3-51)—which is not compatible with either the idea of continuity or curve—the designer has generalized from the experience of other work and distributed shapes on the foundation of a point layout (Figure 3-44) and a continuous diagram

FIGURE 3–52
Labyrinth serpentine drawing.

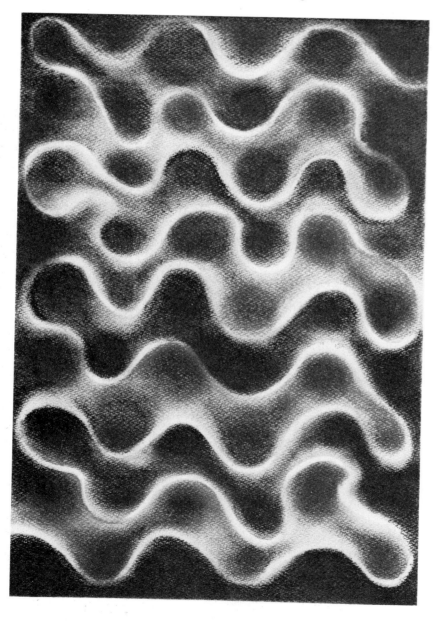

(Figure 3-47) to create the design. The points form centers that control the degree of movement of the line.

VARIATIONS

There are many ways to amplify one Labyrinth framework. A whole series of designs may be created from a single layout by handling it with various drawing techniques, collage, or other media, as well as using the work produced playing Emphasis, or other Composition games, to develop different surfaces. For example, both studies shown in Figures 3-53 and 3-54 use a common framework made up of angles and curves that move toward a center. Done as a pair, each has been rendered in pencil, with emphasis on points and edges in the first, and shaded planes in the second. The result of this graphic manipulation is two surfaces with the same foundation, but with contrast-ing effects. The line of the Labyrinth construction can be tracked in to the center of the plane beginning in the lower left hand corner in the first example, but its exact path has become obscured in the second.

An example of yet another kind of composition based upon a Labyrinth structure is shown in Figure 3-55. It is very complex in its layout, with two continuous lines moving from the center and coiling outward to the edges. The angles have been softened and rounded by developing the surface with tiny dots, shaded from dense to sparse. In addition to the intertwine—which could be likened to the closely packed petals of a flower around its center—there is a subliminal diagonal movement across the surface from lower left to upper right. Combined with the agitation of the angled lines, the three movements—dominated by that of continual unfolding from the center—produces a surface richly varied, but unified through the careful control of movement.

FIGURE 3–53
Labyrinth study. Student project by Nedra Everett, designer.

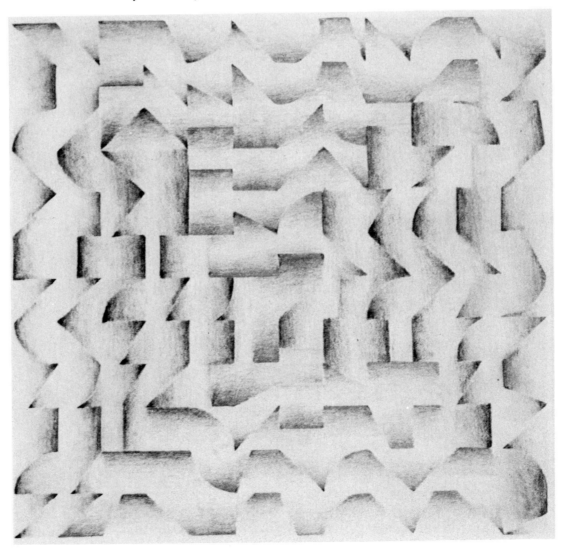

FIGURE 3–54
Labyrinth study, by Nedra Everett.

FIGURE 3–55
Labyrinth study.
Student project by Susan D. Thomas, designer.

COMBINING DESIGN CONCEPTS

Ideas from Manipulation and Scale-change are combined with the structure of a centered Labyrinth framework to create the surface shown in Figure 3-56. A square layout—12 by 12 units—has been combined with a sub-grid of 24 by 24 units. A quarter-circle is the design unit used on the small-scale grid, and a half-circle—or join of two small design units—is used as the design unit on the large-scale grid. Both design units continuously change their positions over the surface: Sometimes they are used singly, sometimes in pairs, in a maze of rotating movements organized on right angles drawn from the interplay of the grids. All of the parts pivot around the center of the composition. The distribution of the simple design elements is skillfully handled, enriching the underlying arrangement of rectangles while revealing it. The dark-light exchange is particularly intriguing: if the light areas are given dominance, shapes of an entirely different character than the quarter- and half-circles can be drawn up from the surface which move through a succession of sizes, all similiar in their general outline, but each different from the other. The piece is an excellent interpretation of the idea of simplicity and variety. The stasis of simple repeat combined with distributed placement is synthesized in a centered compositional framework.

Once the structures evolved from playing Lab-

yrinth have been used and understood, the purpose of the game expands to become one of invention and variation in using them and developing new ones. The player should feel confident and free to invent. As an example, the composition shown in Figure 3-57 is a continuation of ideas already worked through. The basic design is the same as that used in creating the design shown in Figure 3-56—a quarter-circle—from which a number of coordinate shapes have been formed. But the design organization differs. This one is not based on a tightly controlled Labyrinth diagram. It is a deliberate interpretation using closely related but contrasting design elements, arranged in an asymmetrical order. Eight by eight units make a square grid foundation for a discontinuous line diagram which is drawn on more than one edge of the grid unit, as well as crossing its center with a curved line to create the quarter-circles. A further contrast to the preceding example is in the combination of lines and planes in an equilibrium of dark and light shapes. Curves dominate the subordinate right angles; thick and thin elements are freely combined. But the greatest difference between the two examples is in their organizations: Figure 3-56 has elements moving around a center, but by emphasizing certain elements a dominant asymmetrical outlined shape has been drawn around and up from the combined design units that structures the compositional field in Figure 3-57.

FIGURE 3–56
Labyrinth study.

FIGURE 3–57
Labyrinth study.

DESIGN ANALYSIS: SUMMARY SEQUENCE

The sequence of development from Pattern through Distribution to Composition is recapitulated in four plates from a student project: Figures 3-58 through 3-61. Each plate represents an individual interpretation of the forms, all of which are based on a reworking, or manipulation, of the standard grid format. Many variations on the basic game themes are employed in the designs.

To form the grid (Figure 3-58), first a *foundation* grid was established on a rectangular rather than a square unit, and it was left open at the top and bottom edges. Next a *countergrid* of the same line weight was superimposed on the foundation grid, using alternat-

ing intersections of the foundation to coordinate the two. Then a third grid was drawn on the surface in a heavier line weight in an opposing direction to the countergrid, but using the same common intersections from the foundation grid as guide points. This manipulation of the grid structure, done in relation to the right-angled configuration of the foundation grid, creates many shape possibilities depending upon which linear combinations from the new *grid complex* are chosen to be emphasized. This choice is a matter of judgment that must be based upon the experiences of success and failure gained as the result of doing the preceding work.

The hexagon implied in the grid complex surface was selected as the basis for pattern development, the second plate in the sequence (Figure 3-59). Each

FIGURE 3–58
Grid manipulation sequence—grid.

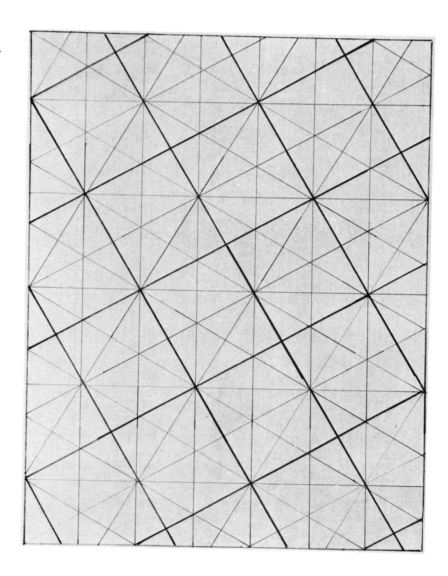

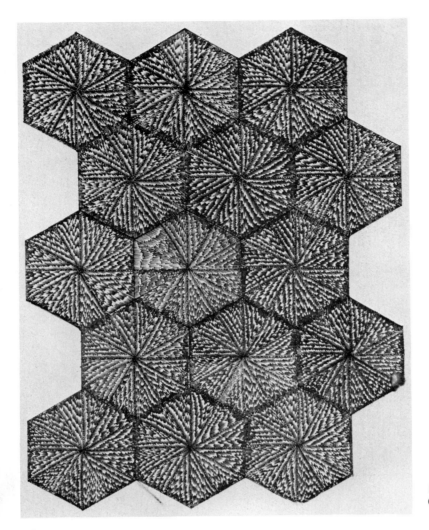

FIGURE 3–59
Grid manipulation sequence—pattern.

complete pattern unit is composed of twelve triangular segments, or sub-units, joined at edges and centers and by common boundaries. Each triangular sub-unit has been heavily rendered with directional texture that appears to rotate around the center point of the hexagon in contrast to the static geometric hexagonal framework.

The interplay of centers, shape edges, and rotating movements produce an active but controlled patterned surface. An intriguing ambiguity in the intention of the design has been introduced by allowing this section of what is obviously a continuous pattern to stand as a single composed unit on a field.

A similar attitude toward the figure-field relationship has been employed in constructing the surface shown in Figure 3-60. The edges of the dominant area give it a specific shape while creating related peripheral shapes that establish various levels of visual activity which function on and within the surface. As a structural basis, irregularly joined triangles, heavily textured with the same staccato markings used in the pattern, are evenly distributed within the framework of the grid complex. A tumbled movement from upper

right to lower right is drawn up from the distributed elements in darker values. Using the same vocabulary of elements formed by the grid manipulation and developed in pattern, the student designer was able to create an entirely new surface from those elements based upon Distribution.

Although the pattern is well realized in its combination of dot, line, and textured shape, it remains well within the framework of a standard static pattern layout. The choice of hexagon as a basis seems nearly arbitrary, given all of the possibilities inherent in the compound relationships of the new and versatile grid structure. The development shown in Figure 3-60 takes full advantage of this versatility and demonstrates a fine control of the surface in doing so. The design units are continually varied and recombined, some units grouped and some emphasized, to create successive centers in the general movement across the surface.

Figures 3-59 and 3-60 should be looked at analytically to compare the similarities and see the contrasts in their forms. What do they have in common? What are their essential differences? The illustrations

122

for basic Pattern and Distribution games should be reviewed from the same standpoint, particularly those examples in which the grid becomes a subordinate element in the finished design, largely or completely absorbed into the developed surface.

The fourth plate in the series, Figure 3-61, is a composition in which an angled asymmetrical figure is evolved from a combination of pattern areas that turn around the support of a dark line—the common boundary of the pattern layout—and the use of value sequence and emphasis. It is an excellent synthesis of the materials drawn from the preceding examples.

The composition reaches out from a clearly defined locus to involve all the areas of the field in an exchange of dark and light shapes that utilize all the complexities of the grid. The pattern basis is stated in lighter values with all parts of the grid structure fully articulated in the same textured triangular segments, common boundaries, and centers used in developing the pattern plate. The dominant figure is based upon the same large rotating movement as that of the third plate, but does not duplicate it, just as the emphasis of area relates to the movement in that example as its basis, but it is not a replication of it.

The grid manipulation shown in Figure 3-58 is the base on which the three examples in this sequence were developed: first, as a pattern in which all lines are given the same weight to create an equally emphasized surface, second, as a distributed surface in which only selected lines are emphasized and carefully controlled in placement; third, as a composition in which the lightly drawn lines of the original grid become subordinate in emphasis to the heavy lines, and the superimposed grid that cants from right to left in the original becomes dominant.

The composition has many levels: some areas advance, others recede. As one studies the surface, the design units combine into dominant asymmetrical shapes, then appear to change to other shapes, while some remain constant as simple pattern passages integrated into the surface. Symmetric and asymmetric modes of balance are synthesized by combining static rhythms and dynamic counter-rhythms, both drawn from the foundation grid. Pattern and Distribution structures are combined in the composition by using the ideas of dominant shape and centered organization—experiences gained by playing Emphasis and

FIGURE 3—60
Grid manipulation sequence—distribution.

FIGURE 3–61
Grid manipulation sequence—composition.

Labyrinth. The visual *organization* of the composition—a balanced interaction of varied movements over the surface—is its *intention*.

DESIGN ANALYSIS: UNIT CONSTRUCTION

The large cloth from Nigeria, shown in Figure 3-62, is made up of narrow woven bands sewn together, a composite technique the same as that used to fabricate the Baule cloth shown in Figure 1-55. Unlike the immediately preceding example of pattern-based composition, Figure 3-61, which expands from a center, the organization here extends vertically up the field with two equal points of concentration aligned diagonally with each other across the center point. All the units of the design are arranged on either side of an obvious center axis, the right and left sides of which are in reverse positions to each other. Such an arrangement might prove uninteresting by itself, but the vertical in the cloth is countered by many small horizontal pulses, placed to accord with the overall symmetry of the piece. These pulses accumulate in a bal-

ancing lateral movement that weaves through the vertical and joins with it. The edges of the field are obscured in close value contrasts and the center emerges from the design units as the contrasts increase and become fully defined in the center groups. As in the preceding plate, centered elements and value control are used to define the composition. Both are beautiful examples of a composition drawn from a pattern-distribution base.

Like most of the materials that have been illustrated, the Nigerian cloth is an example of *unit construction*, the foundation of which is the pattern unit composed within the restriction of the grid—here stated as a compositional organization. Unit construction is not a new idea; it is simply the combination of like elements according to a predetermined system such as Pattern, or an interpretation of such a system in Distribution, or a manipulation of the system as presented in Composition. The common connection between them is the use of a unit and the way it is transformed when it is combined with itself in various relationships.

Although its manifestations may appear extremely complex, the fundamental principle is one of

124

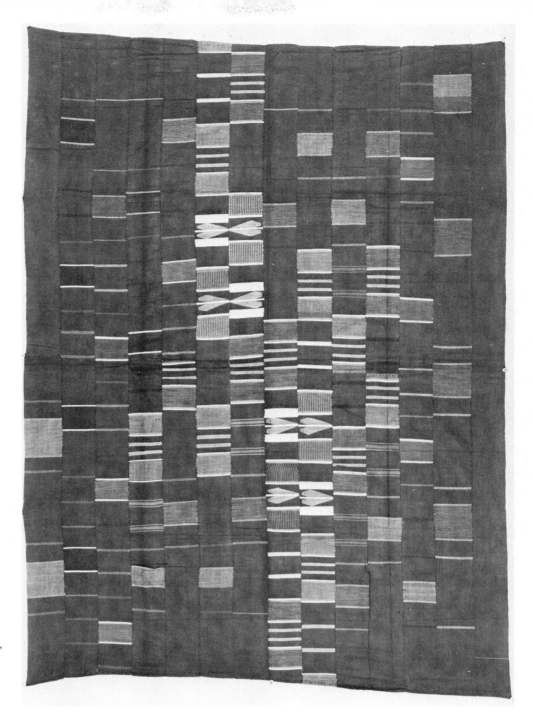

FIGURE 3–62
Men's weave. Yoruba, Oyo,
Nigeria.
Courtesy of The American
Museum of Natural History.

utmost simplicity. Only a single element is used to make the patterned shapes on the East Indian shawl shown in Figure 3-63: a small silver fillet, folded and pressed into the cotton mesh support. By combining these materials with a simple mechanical maneuver, the shawl has been covered with a rich variety of geometric patterns that become even more elaborate and complex when it is draped and worn. The Pakistani embroidered mirror cloth blouse front, Figure 3-64, is composed of small parallelograms and squares in

pattern-like areas that are surrounded by borders placed symmetrically on either side of a long central axis—the center of the garment upon which it is meant to be appliqued. The effect of the uncomplicated arrangement is deceptively ornate. These examples are simple designs, easily understood, in which neither complex shapes nor organizations, but embellishment itself, creates the visual enhancement of familiar primary structures.

Figure 3-65 presents a more complex surface

FIGURE 3–63
Silver shawl from India.

FIGURE 3–64
Pakistani embroidered shirt front.

FIGURE 3–65
Bukhara wall hanging.

126

organization. Originally the lining of a cape from Bukhara, it is seen here used as a flat wall hanging. The complete piece is made up of six separate silk panels of equal width woven from yarns that have been reserve dyed in the *ikat* technique. The method of weaving long bands of fabric and re-assembling them in shorter lengths has been encountered in examples of African textiles. In comparison to the strict grid foundation of the patterns of the Indian shawl, and the symmetry of the Pakistani embroidery, this arrangement seems almost random. It seems too irregular for Distribution and not clearly enough organized for Composition. However, it contains several characteristics of unit construction that relate to both. It is composed of a single dominant element, a large medallion that is regularly spaced on the continuous length of silk by smaller medallions and paired figures. The medallions could just as easily have been put into alignment when the shorter lengths of fabric were arranged to make a straight line across the piece, or placed alternately in succesive rows, but it is just this combination of regular units and irregular spacing—this apparent randomness—that gives the piece its particular interest in the way the visual materials and the method of its organization contrast. Its pattern-like elements are clearly and simply stated, but their arrangement is not: large and small medallions are repetitive, only the paired figures vary from one another to any effective degree. The regular rhythm of the width of the fabric bands paired with the equal size of the medallions give the dominant repetitive support the piece needs to prevent it from becoming visually chaotic. These same factors enhance the contrasts of the irregularities in the vertical spacing. Through the control of the dominant and subordinate elements, a fusion rather than a contradiction is attained, and the medallions appear to move freely up and down in their horizontal track across the surface, grouping, re-grouping, and re-forming themselves in different combinations.

Used for its original purpose, as a cape lining, the piece would have an entirely different meaning than it has as a wall hanging. As bouyant and fresh as the surface appears when seen flat, and as interesting as some of the surface relationships are, it is not a clear statement of composition. Nonetheless the hanging is an expression of one way in which simple design elements may be transformed into larger complexes through their method of joining together.

Although the techniques of *ikat* and assemblage are identical to those used for the Bukhara hanging, the final effect of the four panels that make up the Japanese kimono shown in Figure 3-66 is much different. Here the design has been meticulously layed

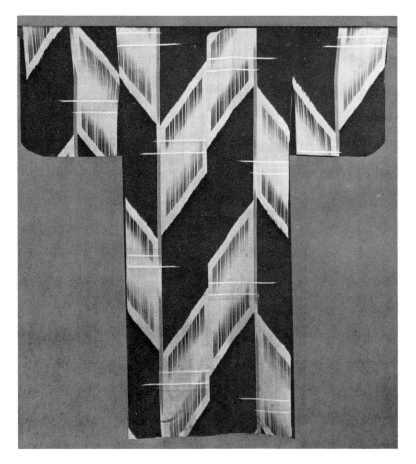

FIGURE 3-66
Japanese kimono.

out beforehand and very little is left to chance placement. The organization is firmly rooted in pattern manipulation combined with a dominant asymmetrical organization on a symmetrical shape. None of the ambiguities of the Bukhara cloth are evident in the kimono. The surface is fully and clearly developed: the dark-light shapes are mutually defining; the strong diagonals are countered by equally strong diagonals in a dynamic exchange between the parallelograms. The total organization is based upon the equal interaction of the dark and the light elements and their powerful movement which is underscored by the elegantly scaled horizontal lines.

The print by the contemporary American artist Peter G. Ramsey, shown in Figure 3-67, may be described as a composition about the union of opposing directions—vertical, horizontal, and diagonal. Compare it with the photograph shown in Figure 3-12, which can be described as a composition about transition from straight to round. Or compare it with the drawing shown in Figure 3-61, which has been described as being about balanced movement. Printed from nine separate metal plates—two triangles, two parallelograms, and five rectangles—the elements used in the Ramsey print would seem too distinct from one another to be brought into any kind of harmonious combination. But the relationships between them have been so skillfully handled that the observer is first aware of the unified effect of the total piece before being led to a study of its parts and how they interrelate.

FIGURE 3–67
Peter G. Ramsey,
Unique print No. 7 (1979).

Essentially symmetrical, all the composing elements are magnetized by the strong horizontal bars cutting across the field slightly below center. The widest of the two bars is exactly centered and cuts the field into an upper and a lower area. The static quality implicit in this kind of placement is alleviated by placing a narrower bar just below it, and, in effect, the two bars join to become one. Rising to the right and left of the upper center bar are two vertical rectangles, their upward motion countered by the reverse grade in the narrower central rectangle which returns and anchors the units to the center. The idea of combining two similiar shapes to make the one shape of the center horizontal rectangle is repeated, in a variation, in the parallelograms in the bottom section of the print, and framed by the repetition of dark triangles. The triangles appear to function as a continuation of the dominant vertical movement of the composition as well as completing its lower horizontal portion.

A series of subtle planar positions is created within the overall surface: the horizontal bar appears forward of the other elements; the central rectangle at the top is positioned behind the bar, but forward from its flanking rectangles. Though not as clearly stated, the dark areas at the bottom appear to belong to still another advancing level. Within the strong right-angled framework of the piece the graded values of the upper rectangles make a soft curved shape which rises and returns to the organizing horizontal rectangle. The vigorously textured areas are drawn in harmony with their supporting shapes, softening and varying them, giving a subordinate contrasting visual richness to the dominant hard angles.

The print and the photograph are the work of individual artists, done independently of each other, and not based on any particular *Graphic Games* structure. However, they are expressions that utilize the disciplines discussed in this book in unique ways, and students of design can use them as two study examples of individual extensions of those disciplines.

DESIGN ANALYSIS: THEMES AND VARIATIONS

All of the games in Composition are open-ended, connected with each other, and capable of being combined. The forms are continually being discovered, developed, reinterpreted and expanded. A point is reached when visual interpretation must become an individual effort that will stand as its own expression, connected to its sources, but offering a unique and particular synthesis: a game played with self-controlled materials within self-created limits.

What follows is a selection of individual designers' variations on the themes of pattern-based composition. They are interspersed with related materials drawn from different sources—some known and some anonymous—along with suggestions for other graphic games that will lead to new surface design structures. It is here, when individuals begin to handle materials in their own ways, that they must make the connections between the foundation games in Pattern, Distribution, and Composition. Some of the organizations will appear familiar; those less familiar should be reviewed in relation to the source illustrations shown throughout the book.

Figure 3-68 is a stitchery done by an advanced design student. It is based on a grid variation, using a rectangle rather than a square as a foundation unit, four across and four down to make a vertical format. On the grid, rectangles are combined with a complex design unit composed of curvilinear elements adapted from Chumash Indian rock paintings. The two are superimposed in a very lively asymmetrical arrangement which centers at the stepped alignment of the dark grid units in the lower center. The plan of this area relates to the reversal seen in Figure 3-62. The curvilinear elements relate to the outlined figure drawn from the surface shown in Figure 3-57. But neither of those design organizations has been duplicated in this composition.

GAME D
SUPERIMPOSITION

Superimposition is a variation on the theme of Combinations—Game C in Chapter 2. This game can be played within the framework of either Pattern, Distribution, or Composition. In it two surfaces, usually

FIGURE 3–68
Student project by Toni Runnels, designer.

of unequal interest, are merged, as in the subordinate rectangle and dominant curvilinear fields shown in Figure 3-68. The new surface is controlled by the rhythmic relationships formed between them, or drawn from the two in combination through emphasis. Or, if the joined surfaces are of equal interest, one or the other, or parts of both can be emphasized to create a unified whole. For example, to continue the theme started in Figure 3-33, Figure 3-69 shows a work sheet in which only outlines have been used to draw the design unit, which has been carefully manipulated so the units combine in a countergrid. This field has then been given a half-turn and superimposed on itself to make the complex of lines shown in Figure 3-70. Some of the lines can be reinforced as dominant and the remainder left as subordinate on the surface as a foundation for several kinds of compositional choices depending upon the designer's need.

The stitchery is a successful, original, and specific use of superimposition—among other things. There is no point in copying it, but there is a point in generalizing from it, and other good examples, to arrive at adaptable forms. Often beginning students set their sights on the target of making an "original" design for no other reason than novelty, or to be "different," and just as often bog down in failure and frustration because they have never defined for themselves the value of doing something different, or why anything should be different in the first place. They have failed

to understand that the new is continually being redefined within the context of the old, the present in terms of the past. Their emphasis is wrongly placed on effects rather than causes, with the production of an exclusive product rather than a development of their own inclusive work process.

Another source of student frustration is that caused by a preoccupation with an idea of what the design was supposed to *be* rather than what it is *becoming*. Persisting in this direction without paying attention to what the work itself is doing, and not responding to its demands as it comes to life, creates a kind of tunnel vision which is a major obstacle to analytic seeing that is very difficult to overcome.

There should never be any hesitancy in using one's own version of a design unit because something resembling it has been used somewhere before, or because someone else has a similar idea in hand. Nor should one draw back from the need to make changes in a design as it is being created, as though such changes are in violation of a pristine and untouchable bright idea. The initiating concept may have been formed in the designer's head, but after the first moves are down on paper the effect has to be assessed and altered in terms of the emerging design rather than being pushed into an unworkable conformity with an inhibiting preoccupation with what the design was "supposed to look like."

The batik shown in Figure 3-71, for example.

FIGURE 3–69
Raven beak design.

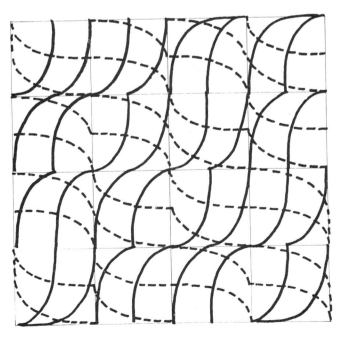

FIGURE 3–70
Raven beak design.

FIGURE 3–71
Student project by Susan D. Thomas, designer.

like the stitchery uses a quarter-circle as its dominant design unit, but much less elaborated, and with an entirely different end result. It has been carefully manipulated, and the value contrasts meticulously placed to produce a surface distinct from that of the stitchery. The contrasts go beyond the effect of particular techniques and into the results of a different ordering of elements. Done by an advanced design student, the layout went through several revisions in preliminary studies using black and white paper, based upon manipulation and emphasis, until the compositional base appeared stable. Further adjustments in value and placement were necessary when the scale of the design units was increased to finished size. The result is a satisfying surface in which the movements created by the joined units are skillfully controlled to continually turn around and into the composition's center of balance.

Compare Figures 3-68 and 3-71. The quarter-circle used in the batik has been reduced to its simplest statement. Although the same shape has been embellished in the stitchery, it has been handled as a simple shape containing and dominating its elaboration. Essentially, both pieces are studies in kinds of movements; the use of the quarter-circle motif appears as more of a contrast than a similarity between the finished pieces.

Another point at which one can founder has already been described, but it is worth reviewing: the overly complicated design unit that is too complete in itself to adapt to combinations. It is always a temptation to manufacture something unnecessarily fancy as an end in itself rather than reducing elements to their simplest possible configurations and allow the relationships between them—the essential composition—to develop their inevitable complexities.

131

COMPOSITION

Only after you have done many preparatory exercises and have analyzed and revised many finished designs should you attempt to use more involved design units. The designer of the batik used the simple motif of a quarter-circle for that composition; then, in a later batik chose to develop a more complex surface. The compound design unit and the organization of the surface are very different from those used in Figure 3-71. The basic shape, a kind of squared off "C" of thick and thin lines, is placed diagonally within the grid unit. Although it divides the unit into several subareas, they are of related 45° and 90° angles and, as can be seen in Figure 3-72, it has been used almost as a countergrid drawn in varying line weights.

Choices such as these, based upon what happens between elements, are what you need to define clearly for yourself in a great deal of preliminary work.

The entire surface is a good example of the interaction of the new shapes created by the proximity of complex primary shapes, but its greatest value as an example is in the interaction of the different scales used. Scale-change and an asymmetrical balance of value contrasts have been combined with a strong biaxial division of the field. Here again, the overall organization of the design, and the interacting of its parts as they relate to and reveal that organization, become more important than the separate design units.

FIGURE 3–72
Student project by Susan D. Thomas, designer.

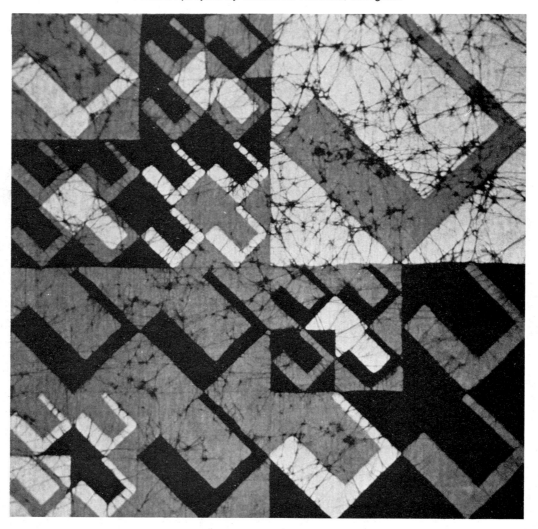

GAME E
COUNTERPOINT

The stitchery and two batiks can further serve to illustrate ways of playing *Counterpoint*, a game that combines design units of one's design played against structures of one's design. The ability to play it at all depends entirely upon understanding the moves and the reasons for them gained from all the other games, since Counterpoint is the confluence of grid basis, design unit, balance, and movement based on the *groundwork* of pattern. The groundwork has been put down and all the necessary diagrams drawn throughout the three chapters. Simply stated, Counterpoint is played with the connections between these elements.

Figures 3-68 and 3-71 have been compared as examples of different kinds of surface movement. In the first, the movement is around and across the surface, countered by the value arrangement of the grid

units; in the second, movements pivot around a center. The first is a more complex example of Counterpoint in which the diverse elements have been unified through their arrangement in a dominant and subordinate order of importance, such as that used in the many examples of combinations of symmetrical and asymmetrical modes of balance that have been shown.

The third example, Figure 3-72, is still more complex. It uses an involved design unit, continuously varied in size and placement to emphasize centers brought up from the surface in a rich asymmetrical interplay structured on the absolutely static foundation of a cross axis. Developing this kind of complexity, drawn from the combinations of all the compositional ways and means, is playing Counterpoint.

The union of opposites, such as the joining of subordinate cross movements within the dominant vertical structure of the Baule cloth (see Figure 1-55) is an integral part of Counterpoint. Another statement of the same basic combination is shown in Figure 3-73, where long is opposed to short, dark to light, vertical to horizontal. The smaller area and size of the

FIGURE 3–73
Men's weave. Akan/Ashanti, Ghana.
Courtesy of The American Museum of Natural History.

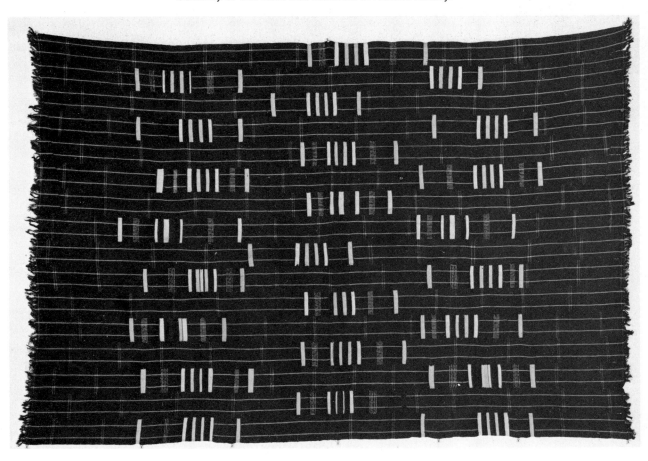

light vertical bars increases their importance in the combination; they become, through contrast, the dominant elements on the plane. Both pieces share a similar pattern base and the same fabrication technique; both combinations establish different spatial levels within the surface. But while the Baule cloth uses an uncentered pattern construction, the Akan/Ashanti cloth emphasizes groups vertically placed to contrast with the general horizontal direction of the weave. In this sense, the two pieces express entirely different surface structures. This kind of contrast, through which seemingly minor elements are transformed to major importance in the design construction, is a salient characteristic of Counterpoint. It can be seen in the counteractions of the grid and linear movements in the stitchery, and the back and forth, stress and release, in the batik based on the angled "C" shape.

Another example in this sequence is the batik shown in Figure 3-74. Here the surface is so active that at first it appears hard to understand. A closer look reveals that it is made up of simple elements, and developed through several familiar steps. Refer to Figure 1-31 to see again how the grid has been absorbed into the action of the pattern; and to Figure 3-14, where new shapes are created out of asymmetrical combinations of the basic shapes, as foundations for this interpretation.

The composition is constructed on the basis of a regular right-angled grid of 36 equal units—6 units across and 6 down. Over this symmetrical framework a line at a 45° angle was drawn from corner to corner across each grid unit, outlining a series of asymmetrically balanced triangles. This new structure was then used to complete a dark-light exchange by dividing each grid unit into a dark triangle and a light triangle. Common edges in dark and light create new shapes—the experience of playing pattern unit manipulation.

The sustaining rhythm is that of diagonal descending movements countered by ascending movements. As a counterpoint to the massed triangular design units that make interacting shapes in the composition, a line has been drawn parallel to the long side of the triangle which becomes an aligning axis for three small squares. These sub-units are placed in conformity with the positions of the triangular design units, but in reverse values. They join at common edges to make further subordinate contrasting rectangular and right-angled shapes. Two scales have been joined that add considerable vitality to the surface as well as giving it greater depth. Throughout, the elements are encompassed within their organization—which is a fusion of their contrasts—in a union of simple design elements and complex surface structure.

FIGURE 3–74
Chris Baumgartner, designer.

GAME F
INDIVIDUAL INTERPRETATION

As one works through different forms of surface organization the finished pieces become examples which originate other ideas, and suggest possibilities of new combinations. Basic forms are recognized in designs from many sources and become accessible for analysis and reinterpretation within the frame of reference of one's own work. Upon analysis, designs that at first seem dissimiliar are discovered to have common connections in the ordering of their relationships.

For example, the Chinese embroidered panel shown in Figure 3-75 contains a treasure of patterns in a lively arrangement, although the scenario of court life may appear nearly meaningless to a contemporary observer. Set up in a rough symmetry and centered on the lower dark-robed figure, the panel is made up of several naively arranged separate scenes unified within the horizontal framework of four wide bands, or units. Without the rhythm of the large-to-small, large-to-small sequence from top to bottom, the piece would become a scattering of miscellaneous effects without an organizational point. The banded construction is the point. It has been seen, with variations, in Japanese *kata-gami*, African textiles, the Bukhara

FIGURE 3–75.
Embroidered Textile, Chinese.
Courtesy of The Seattle Art Museum, Eugene Fuller Memorial Collection.

hanging, and other examples. It is so basic an idea that it cannot be copied, but only interpreted. The figures moving in their hierarchical order through the horizontals in the court scene is a particular expression, but the banded idea is not—nor is the idea of asymmetrical placement of the figures within the bands. The designer of the batik (Figure 3-74) has interpreted this general idea by placing the small-scale figures firmly within the context of the larger, dominant units of the design.

The same designer has interpreted the idea of horizontal banding by combining it with a symmetrical scale-change to organize the strongly structured surface of the batik wall hanging shown in Figure 3-76.

The preliminary work sheet for the design is shown in Figure 3-77—the finished piece deviates slightly in the details, but the basic setup remains the same—and clarifies the method of changing scale from small to double, then double again. The order is then reversed. Within each of the five areas the positions of the triangles is determined in the same way used in planning the composition shown in Figure 3-74. The difference is in the position of the darks and lights—placed to minimize joins that would create larger complex shapes—which allows the triangles to maintain their identity as distributed elements. This deliberate asymmetrical joining creates a counterpoint of changing directions over the surface which plays against the

FIGURE 3–76
Chris Baumgartner, designer.

FIGURE 3–77
Worksheet for Figure 3–76.

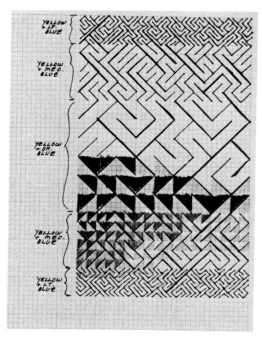

GAME F: INDIVIDUAL INTERPRETATION

uniform rhythm of the changes in size. The counter-rhythms of pause and flow and the simplicity of the order of the areas combine in a beautifully balanced surface that is as effective when seen vertically as it is when seen horizontally.

One of the richest surfaces in our sequence of examples is that of the batik shown in Figure 3-78. It first appears as an organization drawn from Labyrinth, but in fact the basic maneuvers are drawn from Figures 3-74 and 3-76, and arranged as rotations around an approximate center in the square surface. The design unit, a simple one made up of two triangles within the grid unit each broken into five bars with values reversed from side to side, is symmetrically manipulated within the grid foundation. The intriguing parts of the surface construction lie in the manner in which the edges of the joined triangles are emphasized with a line that is counter in scale and value to the heavier lines on the body of the triangle, and the distribution of the value reversals. In the subtlest possible way, the design has drawn up interlocked shapes that are heavily and consistently figured, but seem to position themselves slightly above, then slightly below their neighboring shapes in a constant fluctutation. The larger scale figure has been reduced to a subordinate function, and the thinner line thrown up into shape controlling relief through contrast.

Figure 3-79 should be compared with Figures

FIGURE 3–78
Chris Baumgartner, designer.

COMPOSITION

3-74 and 3-78. By the same designer, the three pieces can be seen as a suite of variations on a common theme of centralized organization. This, the final piece in the series, is of stencil dyed and stitched fabric. The grid units are doubled to make a rectangular design unit containing three light curved lines, and a dark triangle. The units are placed in a full rotation around a clearly stated center in an arrangement of opposing diagonals. The organization needs little explanation—it is at once simple and dynamic.

The extraordinary surface of Figure 3-80 was created by the contemporary Japanese artist Masakatsu Ueda. Using a puncturing device of his own invention, which looks like a small bed of nails, pointed steel pins are positioned on a predrilled, heavy flat board in various arrangements to serve as a regular grid foundation. Very stiff handmade paper is then placed over the sharp points of the pins and pressed firmly down onto them with the aid of a top board drilled through with holes matching those of the bot-

FIGURE 3–79
Chris Baumgartner, designer.

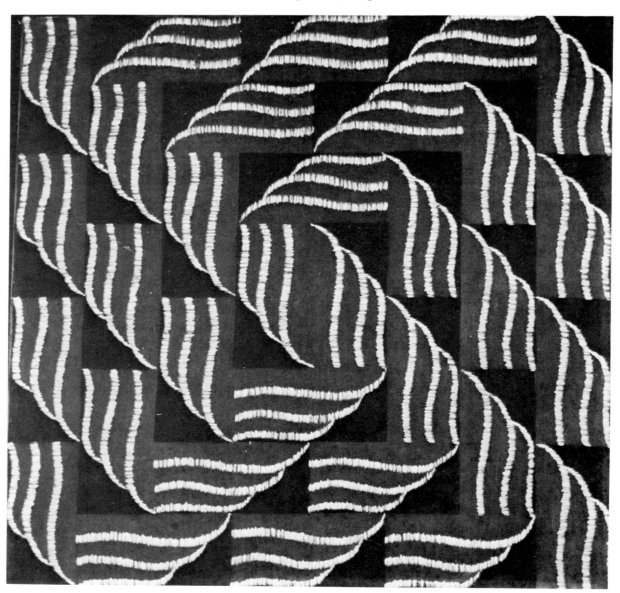

tom piece. The results are compositions that use variations of grid arrangements as their subject.

The paper can be repositioned and perforated again or, as in the example shown in Figure 3-80, "Perfographic No. 5," turned over so that the torn edge of the puncture is in relief on one side or the other. Very little is left to chance in the manipulation of tool and material: the results are calculated on variations that can be drawn from the grid combinations. "Perfographic No. 5" shifts one 10 by 10 grid down and over two units, increasing the overall area to 12 by 12 units. The two grids are superimposed on each other in a slight shift away from a 90° angle alignment.

The paper has been perforated from the front and from the back.

The surface is elusive: it comes and goes, sometimes appearing as a simple arrangement of dots, then as merged squares. Areas of concentration fluctuate over the field. Then the contrasting movement caused by the slight off-right angle placement curves across its center bringing a new visual meaning out of the joined grid units. Using an absolute economy of means, the artist has skillfully structured an evocative surface from the simplest visual materials, a surface that goes beyond a mere combination to reveal a new form in the relationship of its composing elements.

FIGURE 3–80
Masakatsu Ueda, Perfographic No. 5.

CONCLUSION

FROM PATTERN
TO COMPOSITION

Raven screen. Huna, Tlingit; Northwest Coast Indian.
Red and black paint on cedar boards.
© Courtesy of the Denver Art Museum,
Denver, Colorado.

Must all compositions be based on a grid? Of course not. There are hundreds of compositions that make no obvious reference to a grid as an organizing foundation, although they certainly may be built upon foundations that relate directly to many of the structures and the design factors discussed—movement, dominant and subordinate orders of visual interest, interacting rhythms—perhaps organized in less metrical ways, but nonetheless organized in some comprehensible manner which is the essential part of the larger definition of composition that has been given.

So why insist on the grid? The grid provides designers—especially beginners—a working basis for organization in two-dimensional design. The grid provides a stand upon which the impulse to create can flourish in an ordered and productive manner. It is used to establish the design structures in pattern that make the foundation for composition. This is far more easily done by using a controllable unit, with relationships unfolding from unit to unit, until the whole is revealed, rather than having to face the awesome prospect of dealing with a blank page at the start of the design process. The grid should be used as it has been used throughout the games: as a basis for interpretation, and first for Pattern, which is the defining structure from which Distribution and Composition evolve. Used in this manner—as a means and not an end—the grid becomes a way of gaining freedom of control rather than a restriction.

The key game in Pattern is "Manipulations." It establishes the basis for all subsequent work in graphic games, that of dealing with the visual materials one has invented through simple to complex pattern structures. Any of the examples shown in the chapters on Composition and Distribution can be analyzed from the standpoint of their pattern basis and how it extends to composition. Many of the pattern examples become compositional in content as they become more complex.

Pattern, Distribution, and Composition are all aspects of the same thing, the same kind of approach to the surface: manipulating a pattern foundation; and working with a grid is the basis of that. But once the foundation has been achieved, the freedom to experiment and discover new ways of using it are at hand, and the possibilities for individual creation—controlled and purposeful work, not happy accidents—open up.

While writing the chapter on Composition I became aware that I was leaving out parts of the material that I had collected while teaching the subject because the chapter was running on and on. To come to a conclusion seemed impossible since work doesn't proceed in a straight line from start to finish but rather in a series of continually expanding circles. "Well," I thought, as I cut back, amended, or re-wrote, "the important point is the *connections*; if design students

Peruvian clay pot.
Provenance unknown.

141

get that then they will want to continue on their own and develop more themselves." There is in fact no end to the subject. It goes on being explored and expanded in the work of committed artists.

In so many ways art is an eminently practical matter. The artist is always preoccupied with the pragmatics of getting an idea down so it will communicate the meaning of its inner relationships—its sensible order. That is why this book uses the games approach, challenging you to work out your individual solutions. The method will not succeed if you merely repeat the exercises by rote. The work must be combined with thought and feeling. Use the exercises as a springboard; let the examples stimulate you to finding new moves that work. After you have played the games for a while the moment will come when you will exclaim, "A-ha! Of course. But *I* can do it *this* way." And that is the way to win.

DATE DUE

FEB 6 '89			
GAYLORD			PRINTED IN U.S.A.